MYTHS OF ANCIENT EGYPT

For Clara

MYTHS OF ANCIENT EGYPT

GODS AND PHARAOHS, CREATION AND THE AFTERLIFE

CATHERINE CHAMBERS

amber
BOOKS

Published by
Amber Books Ltd
United House
North Road
London
N7 9DP
United Kingdom
www.amberbooks.co.uk
Instagram: amberbooksltd
Facebook: www.facebook.com/amberbooks
Twitter: @amberbooks

ISBN: 978-1-78274-920-2

Project Editor: Sarah Uttridge
Designer: Hart Mcleod Ltd
Picture Research: Terry Forshaw

Printed in China

1 4 6 8 10 9 7 5 3 2

CONTENTS

INTRODUCTION

Ancient Egypt's vast, complex mythology evolved in a context of dramatic natural forces that blessed the region with food and wealth, and that seemed like miracles to the early inhabitants of this northeast corner of Africa.

Here, from around 8000 BCE, bordered by a huge and fast-desiccating environment, a sanctuary had opened up in the delta and lower reaches of the River Nile. Following the gradual desertification of North Africa's savannah grasslands, farmers and pastoralists had migrated to this greener, sparsely inhabited spot, pushed beyond what became the inhospitable Sahara.

By about 6000 BCE, small settlements had developed into walled towns, sustained by oases both in the delta and in the Western Desert and by narrow strips of cultivable land that hugged the Nile. These urban areas flourished as wealth grew from surpluses traded across desert and sea, and along the Nile's long navigable stretch. It was on the banks of this great river that the annual miracle of inundation occurred, around which many of Ancient Egypt's gods, their stories and their powers were created.

From miracle to myth
According to myth, Hapi, the god of the Nile flood and Lord of the Fish and Birds of the Marshes, lives by the First Cataract, a

OPPOSITE: On a wall at Dendera Temple near Qena, just north of Luxor, a priest makes an offering to Hapi, whose lotus flower headwear shows that he is god of the Nile.

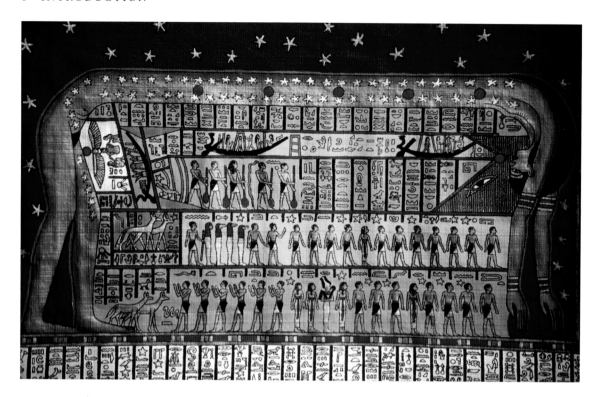

ABOVE: **A traditional portrayal of celestial goddess, Nut, shows her as a vault overarching the earth. This is a papyrus copy from a Late Period temple at Dendera.**

great waterfall near modern-day Aswan. Every year, he travels through the heavens, then crosses through Duat, the land of the dead, reappearing miraculously through a mountain cave.

This epic journey describes the annual inundation of the Nile, which sustained a rich agricultural economy close to the harsh Sahara. Every year, Ancient Egyptians endured searing heat from mid-June to September, waiting for the bulging clouds from the south to burst over the Ethiopian Highlands, sending cascades of water into streams that fed the Nile. With these waters came the added blessing of nutrients, washed down by Sudan's White Nile, which flowed into the Blue Nile at Khartoum and northward to the delta. As the waters receded, a black, fertile, silty soil, several metres deep, was left behind. From November, the land was drained well enough for the sowing and growing season, *peret*, to begin. By April, crops were ripe and ready for *shemu*, harvest time. All this was made possible by *akhet*, the annual flood.

An auspicious star

At the same time that Ancient Egyptians witnessed the wonder of *akhet*, the bright star, Sirius, personified by the goddess Sopdet, heralded the annual flood's arrival. Together, the star and the waters were praised in most years as god-given blessings. In a low floodwater year, when famine hit, or a high floodwater year, when all was washed away, they were marked as a punishing curse. Either way, Ancient Egyptians were helpless in the face of the forces of nature, which were controlled by gods whose power was narrated through their myths.

The rising sun and the risen dead

At least as important as these annual natural events was the daily life of the sun, which used its power to transform seedlings into abundant crops when the flood succeeded, yet shrivelled them when it failed. For Ancient Egyptians, this uncertainty was compounded by the sun's disappearance at night, inducing anxiety that it would fail to reappear the next day.

Only deities such as Nut could ensure the perpetuation of the sun's daily rhythm. A goddess of the stars and sky, Nut swallows the evening sun, which makes its way through her body to be reborn the following morning.

The daily cycle of the sun mirrored the passing of human beings from life to death, and raised the great question of the existence of an afterlife. Among the pantheon of powerful gods emerged those who could guide the living through their time on earth, in both calm and chaos, and those who could steer them in an ethereal barge through Duat, the underworld, to reincarnation. If judged fit to travel along this journey beset by obstacles, the deceased could aim for Aaru, the Field of Reeds. This was a paradise that mirrored life on earth at its best. In dynastic times, it was ruled over by Osiris, god of the sun at night, of the Nile reeds and of rebirth.

Towards a national mythology

From 6000 to 3150 BCE, under the gaze of early creator deities, and others more local and personal, farmers hoed and sowed in the damp, fertile land, irrigating staple foods such as wheat and barley by means of manmade water channels and the *shaduf*, a hand-operated irrigation tool. Abundant fodder supported domesticated sheep, goats, pigs and donkeys. The Nile waters supplied fish, as well as reeds for boats, houses and writing pens.

ABOVE: **A star tops the head of Sopdet, or Sothis, goddess of Sirius.**

ABOVE: **Luxor's vast Karnak temple complex, dedicated principally to Amun, was built through Egypt's wealth on top of a small ancient site dated about 3400 BCE.**

They sustained crops of the papyrus plant, with its many uses, from roots for food to stalks for small skiffs and pith for paper. Surplus produce was traded for precious metals, gems, ivory and woods. Wealth grew, the population increased, rulers surfaced to control it all, and a pantheon of powerful gods with complex narratives emerged to strengthen the rulers' grip on their territory.

A material culture developed in which arts and crafts became increasingly sophisticated, and were used by Ancient Egyptians to express their devotion to gods through carved, etched and moulded artefacts. After a united dynastic Egypt emerged between 3100 and 2686 BCE, signs and symbols developed into a written language that facilitated not only the nation's vast documentation of administrative records, accounts and diplomatic correspondence, but also the depiction and description of a swelling pantheon of gods and their roles in myth.

The greatest myth of all was that the power of deities was independent of pharaohs and high priests and priestesses who, until the First Intermediate Period (c. 2160–2055 BCE), controlled the temples that enshrined these multifaceted gods and their myths.

CHRONOLOGY

Palaeolithic Period	c. 700,000–7000 BCE
Saharan Neolithic Period	c. 8800–4700 BCE
Predynastic Period	c. 5300–3000 BCE
Early Dynastic Period	c. 3000–2686 BCE
Old Kingdom	2686–2160 BCE
First Intermediate Period	2160–2055 BCE
Middle Kingdom	2055–1650 BCE
Second Intermediate Period	1650–1550 BCE
New Kingdom	1550–1069 BCE
Ramessid Period	1295–1069 BCE
Third Intermediate Period	1069–664 BCE
Late Period	664–332 BCE
Ptolemaic Period	332–30 BCE
Roman Period	30 BCE – AD 395

1

MYTHS IN SCULPTURE, SIGN, SYMBOL AND SCRIPT

Ancient Egypt's myths, like those of other African cultures, were ancient oral traditions that adapted and changed over thousands of years. So although the gods became the subjects of artworks and script, most Ancient Egyptians could hold their narratives in their heads.

Stories of Ancient Egypt's gods explained life's big questions, such as who created the earth, the forces of nature, abundant or failed harvests, and tussles between order and chaos or good and evil. They were so well known that it was not necessary to depict them or write them down in their entirety. Fragments of myths and gods and, more often, mere allusions to them through a symbol or an iconic depiction, were usually all that were required for an Ancient Egyptian to recognize the myth, its context,

OPPOSITE: **A basalt statue of Horus at Edfu Temple built between 237 and 57 BCE shows that his power lasted from predynastic times to the end of the kingdom.**

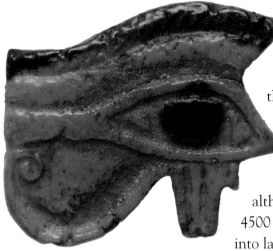

ABOVE: This Eye of Horus, or 'wedjat' amulet is made of turquoise; the colour symbolizes protection. Horus's eyes were the sun and the moon.

meaning and function. Implicitly, these fragments could also infer the roles of other gods associated with the myth in question, and each god's characteristics and status within the pantheon.

Towns and their totems

Predynastic archaeological finds depicting mythical beings have been dated to 4000 BCE, although some early totems date back to at least 4500 BCE. At this time, small settlements had grown into large villages and then bustling trading towns. Here, a middle class with wealth to spare had spawned communities of craftspeople who made everything from furniture and cooking vessels to figurines and amulets.

Sacred images and forms were painted, carved or etched from simple materials such as wood, ivory tablets or ostraca (broken pieces of shell or limestone, or potsherds). These were fashioned not only as domestic votive items but also as burial goods, showing an early preoccupation with the role of gods and their myths in smoothing the way into an afterlife.

Between 4000 and 3500 BCE, the number of grave goods found in high-status tombs escalated sharply. Even in those predynastic times, these tombs could be large, opulent and marked out by their elaborate wooden roofs, remnants of which have been preserved in the dry desert heat. Importantly, grave goods included totems with images of gods whose powerful roles in myth continued into dynastic times.

Most of these finds, dating from about 3790 to 3640 BCE, have been unearthed in burial sites around the southern city of Hierakonpolis, also known as Nekhen. Here, archaeologists have found the first above-ground evidence of funerary temples, as well as burial sites not only for humans but also for animals, from dogs to elephants.

Humans found in a high-status burial site were killed to accompany their master into the afterlife to meet his daily needs. Faith was not quite strong enough to trust that the gods would provide. But among the bones, limestone statuettes, cosmetic slate palettes for applying kohl eye make-up, carved ostrich eggs and knapped flint artefacts have been unearthed. Also found were crafted symbols of powerful totems such as the hippopotamus.

In March 2014, archaeologists discovered a young man of high status, possibly the son of a local leader, buried in Tomb 72, alongside 54 separate items. Among these were hippo-headed combs, an ivory wand carved along the top with a parade of hippopotami and a hippo figurine fashioned from soapstone. All were trumped by a 32cm (12½in) long hippo tooth, carved in the form of a bearded man with large ears, perhaps connecting the strength of the hippopotamus's narrative with that of its human owner.

Linking myth with power

We do not know the exact association between early hippopotamus totems, their mythical status and their adoption by powerful humans. However, later evidence in the *Book of the Dead* (c. 1500 BCE) suggests that the hippopotamus's ferocity and stature led to its position in the pantheon as one animal aspect

BELOW: These finds at Tomb 72 in Hierakonpolis include a hippo-topped comb and, at the bottom left, the hippo tooth figurine.

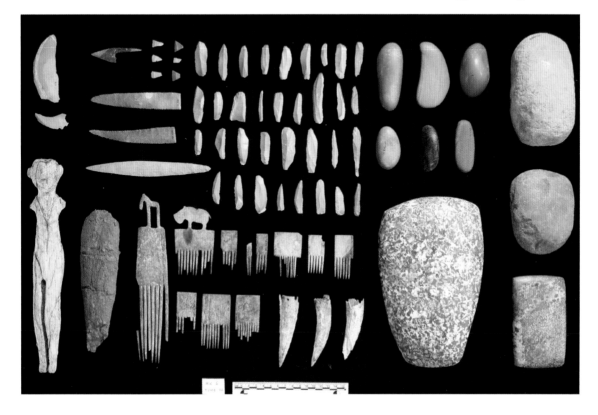

of the goddess Taweret. Her mythical roles included protecting the annual flood, particularly at a point where the waters gushed down with great force at Gebel el-Silsila, just north of modern-day Aswan. As a bringer of bounty, she was naturally associated with fertility and childbearing. Later still, Taweret's strength enabled her to guard the mythical pathways in the western mountains, where she used magic spells to ease a deceased person's journey through the perils of the underworld.

Taweret's mythical journey from powerful but simple icon to complex deity was a typical trajectory for ancient gods that began as creature icons. The falcon was a case in point. In this same Tomb 72, the earliest discovery of a falcon-shaped totem was made, beautifully crafted from green malachite. Most probably it was an early image of Horus, the god of kings.

Myth and the unification of Egypt

One of the earliest creator gods, falcon-headed Horus emerged in myth from a world engulfed in darkness and chaos, where the earth was a swill of silt and water. From a murky sky, Horus flew down and perched on a reed that arose straight and strong from the marshland at the edge of a muddy island. Humans surfaced from the small mound of land to build protective walls around the sacred falcon, and so a protected community with a deity was formed in the land that became Egypt.

This ancient creation myth is not the only reason why Horus was an early totem. As a raptor, he was also a symbol of power and speed, and had ferocious weaponry at his disposal. It is not surprising, therefore, that among early finds in high-status tombs there are artefacts with the Horus head or symbol.

More importantly, as the predynastic era faded in the face of Ancient Egypt's momentous period of unification, Horus's protective walls became symbolized as an urban centre controlled by a king, incorporated into

one of the earliest hieroglyphs. This was found on the Bull
Palette (c. 3200–3000 BCE), featuring the symbolism of the
bull itself, which became one of the five powerful names of
the king, as did Horus. At this time, myth became a powerful
tool in the jostle for supremacy among Upper Egypt's growing
city-states, as the region was poised to take over the delta
towns of Lower Egypt. Kings were not shy in alluding to their
mythical power in artworks, tombs and on weapons.

Myth, mythical power and unification

By about 3500 BCE, provinces called *sepat*, later renamed
nomes by the Greeks, had formed a patchwork of separate
power bases across Ancient Egypt. Each was ruled by a
nomarch who sported regalia that included symbols of their
great patron god. The Horus kings of Upper Egypt in the
north, based at the cities of Thinis, Nekhen (Hierakonpolis)
and Naqada in Upper Egypt, south of
Aswan, jostled for power during this later
predynastic time, until Thinis triumphed
by around 3150 BCE.

Thereafter, the region entered a murky
period in which an empowered Upper Egypt
gained control of Lower Egypt. Possibly
it was by conquest, as evidenced by the
triumphal scenes on the Narmer Palette,
an engraved, shield-shaped ceremonial
stele made of siltstone and unearthed from
the temple floor in the Main Deposit of
the Nekhen (Hierakonpolis) necropolis.
Yet a unification achieved through battle
might be allegorical, and Lower Egypt
could just as well have been overcome
gradually, through the economic supremacy
of the prosperous southern city-states.

RIGHT: **An example of the long-lasting royal
cartouche at the New Kingdom Temple of
Rameses III.**

The gods endorse the first king

Between 1897 and 1898, two British archaeologists, James Quibell and Frederick Green, unearthed one of the earliest historical documents in the world. The Narmer Palette, intricately carved on grey-green siltstone and standing at 64cm (25in) tall, bears witness to the gods' validation of the first king of Egypt. Hieroglyphs name him as Narmer: 'n'r', the sound and symbol for the catfish, and 'mr', meaning a chisel. Engraved in shallow relief on both sides, the palette was never intended for mixing cosmetics but as a ceremonial piece. It has been dated

THE SECOND TEMPLE AT NEKHEN

The Main Deposit of finds is located in the second, mainly Early Dynasty (3000–2686 BCE) temple at Nekhen, which was built around an even older sacred mound. The Nekhen complex was so important to rulers that renovations and additions continued at least to the Middle Kingdom (2055–1650 BCE). The Main Deposit, so rich in finds, was unearthed within stone walls constructed during the Old Kingdom (2686–2160 BCE). But a fine golden falcon god statue of Nekheny, probably a precursor to Horus, was dug up within a clay brick structure from the Middle Kingdom.

Whatever the means, Upper Egypt, embodied by Horus and the vulture goddess, Nekhbet, defeated Set, a beast of unidentifiable species and the god of Lower Egypt, who was partnered by the snake goddess, Wadjet. The mythical stories and powers of these gods and goddesses were embodied not only in their images but also in the crowns of the two regions.

ABOVE: **A single obsidian rod forms the black eyes of Horus, god of the Nekhen Temple.**

Deshret, 'the red one', describes the red crown of the delta city of Nubt, the City of Gold, and of both Wadjet and Set. This god of chaos and murderous intent nevertheless flashed occasional glimpses of a more benign deity down through the dynasties. Deshret was evinced by a predynastic potsherd broken from a large vessel with a raised red crown on it. This represented a bloody and outrageous Set, who in myth slaughtered his own brother Osiris. Osiris, a most favoured deity, was rescued from his doomed life in the underworld by the actions of his wife, Isis, and thus became a mighty god of the afterlife.

In the south, Hedjet, the white crown of Horus and Nekhbet, was also known as 'the bright one'. This saviour-like image seemed to represent aptly an upright Horus king defeating the devious Set king. When unification was achieved, the crowns were carved separately, one on each side of the Narmer Palette, and later together on the crowns of successive kings of united Egypt.

to about 3150 BCE along with other finds at Nekhen (Hierakonpolis) commemorating unification in the Temple of Horus.

A frieze runs across the top of each side of the palette, featuring either bulls or cows, perhaps symbolizing the god Apis or the goddess Hathor. Know as the sky goddess 'of many names', Hathor was also the consort of Horus, so was closely identified with the king of unification and those who succeeded him. Along the bottom of one side of the palette lie the slain of Lower Egypt; on the other, a bull breaks down a city's walls with its horns and crushes a defeated enemy soldier with its hooves. The bull, though unnamed, was possibly the bull-headed god Apis, one of the great gods of Memphis, which became the capital of Egypt during the First Dynasty.

Both sides of the palette indicate that unification was achieved through decisive military force. On one side, Narmer is preceded by four bearers proudly carrying standards on tall flagpoles, which include a representation of Wepwawet, god of the 'opening of the ways', possibly symbolizing his divine assistance in clearing a path to a unified Egypt. This jackal-headed (some say wolf-headed) god is a protector of the dead, ensuring that they conquer all obstacles on their way to a glorious afterlife.

On the other side, Narmer strikes a heavy blow with a club upon his enemy, while Horus, the falcon god of Upper Egypt and legitimizer of kings, hovers triumphantly over the subjugated delta wetlands. One talon rests on papyrus plants while the other, shaped as a hand, clutches a rope that pulls on the head of an unfortunate prisoner.

RIGHT: **The Narmer Palette's shield shape represents power. It is a ceremonial makeup palette with a mixing cupola cupped by protective snake-necked lions.**

THE DOUBLE CROWN

Known as the Pschent, the double crown worn throughout the dynasties represented not only a unified Egypt but also the interplay between power, politics, gods and myths. The crowns were sometimes embellished with the upright cobra, the Uraeus, of the northern goddess Wadjet, together with the vulture of the southern goddess Nekhbet. At times they were depicted on top of Horus, as above, to reinforce unification under a southern king.

The mythology of the first king

It was the unification of Egypt that enabled a patchwork of city-states, each with its own totemic god, to expand into a theocracy with a national religion and mythology, although regional gods kept their place. Unification elevated some gods and the stories around them over others, a process that continued as dynasties came and went.

In the turmoil of unification, myths have shifted around the identity of the king of unification himself. The Narmer Palette points firmly to Narmer, a Horus king, as the first ruler of a united Ancient Egypt, and one blessed by the gods. He is also inscribed at the top of King Lists found in the tombs of subsequent rulers, Den and Qa'a of the First Dynasty, at Abydos, the royal necropolis for Nekhen (Hierakonpolis).

Narmer's was not the only name in the mix, although names might be mere epithets. Unification may have been achieved through gradual change mythologized as a single dramatic and conclusive event rather than as a process achieved possibly through trade and treaty. Therefore, the identity of the true first ruler of a unified Egypt still hovers in a liminal space. More than one person might have vied to be written into history and mythology as the first divine king of Egypt. It seems that only the gods' positions remain certain at this point.

Hor Aha – the first true King of Egypt?

Hor Aha, whose name, Fighting Falcon, symbolizes the strength and nobility of Horus, was declared the first king on an ivory label unearthed at Saqqara, the necropolis for Memphis, which became the new capital of a unified Egypt during the First Dynasty. Yet he was described as only the second king after Narmer on a sandy-clay jar seal sherd engraved with falcons surmounting serekhs (ornamental vignettes) unearthed from Umm el-Qa'ab cemetery at the Abydos burial site. It is thought that he was most probably the son of Narmer and his consort, Neithotep, and therefore inherited the throne after Narmer's death.

Menes – king or characteristic?

The name of King Menes, which means 'he who endures', was engraved on an ivory label along with that of Hor Aha in a Naqada tomb. Later, he was cited as the first king on both the Turin King List (1275–1200 BCE) and the Abydos King List (c. 1290–1279 BCE), and was put forward by the Ptolemaic priest and historian Manetho (c. 300 BCE), who used as evidence the King List inscribed on the Palermo Stone (Old Kingdom). However, many Egyptologists believe that Menes is just another name for Narmer or Hor Aha, describing the tenacious qualities of whoever was the true unifier.

BELOW: **A fragment of the black basalt Palermo Stone king list.**

THE EXCAVATIONS OF JAMES QUIBELL (1867–1935)

James Quibell was the first Egyptologist to recognize that finds dated well before the Fourth Dynasty, as was previously thought. He based his theory on excavations at Naqada cemeteries, which he suggested were predynastic rather than from the Intermediate Period. Finds from several predynastic periods at Naqada are used to help date those from other sites. Quibell's important discoveries included papyri and artefacts used for spells and medicine, linked to the powers of the gods and found in tomb shafts of the mortuary temple of Rameses II (1279–1213 BCE).

BELOW: **A copy of early hieroglyphic text from the Ebony Tablet of Menes (c. 3400 BCE).**

If Ancient Egyptian king-naming follows a tradition across much of Africa – one in which multiple praise names are showered on rulers and woven into their oral genealogies – then the idea that Narmer or Hor Aha and Menes are the same person is not improbable. The multifaceted nature of such a great change-maker is in line with the many aspects of the gods, and again in tune with leadership and belief systems across the continent.

BELOW: **A copy of early hieroglyphic text from the Ebony Tablet of Menes (c. 3400 BCE).**

The Scorpion King

Overarching these contenders is the Scorpion King, who could be either a character or a concept. The scorpion's menacing image was portrayed as symbols on two substantial ceremonial carved limestone maceheads, unearthed close to the Narmer Palette. On the smaller macehead, a scorpion motif and a rosette by the red-crowned king's head seems to lead him as he wields a flail, with Horus, holding a rope, facing him.

Was the flail for thrashing grain, showing the king as a provider, or more ambiguously for use as a weapon? Was 'scorpion' an epithet for the stinging, incisive power of the king? Or did the scorpion image show that the unifier was protected and endorsed, perhaps by the scorpion goddess Selket?

Fragile kingdom; constant gods

According to current evidence, the first few rulers did not in fact claim to be the kings of both Upper and Lower Egypt, yet Horus's constant and often bold image shows that he reigned supreme as the divine national god, and the dual red and white crowns appear consistently as insignia. Possibly, the hold on both territories was at times tenuous. It was Den – also known as the Horus name of Hor-Den, an early king of the First Dynasty (3150–2686 BCE), either the third or fourth – who was the first to declare himself without hesitation as the king of both regions. He confirmed his position by being also the first to use the royal name 'King of the sut plant and the bee', uniting the sedge grass of Upper Egypt with the bee of Lower Egypt, and the warring gods Horus and Set, who are depicted together in some of the imagery associated with Den.

BELOW: An ebony oil jar label from about 3000 BCE shows the names of King Den, his official seal bearer, Hemaka, and another official, Iti-sen.

THE LARGER SCORPION MACEHEAD

The Larger Scorpion Macehead shows the king wearing a white crown and a bull's tail. A scorpion motif and a rosette are carved beside his head. He is standing near an irrigation canal that is perhaps being dug or cleared by workmen; another symbol of the king's benign will to feed his people. Yet there is also a row of standards representing different *nomes* with dead birds strung from them, dangling by their necks.

Selket, an ancient, powerful and often valiant scorpion goddess, protected the greatest gods and therefore could, by extension, be a protector of the kings of unification. Among the many mythical roles associated with Selket is her continual, unresolved battle with the great snake devil, Apep. This malevolent god's relentless mission to destroy the vital process of reincarnation was played out on a daily basis as he tried to prevent Re, the god of the sun and reincarnation, from rising at dawn.

Like many of the weaponized deities, Selket's actions were not always benevolent, so she was feared as well as welcomed. Her duality is manifested in her two contrasting symbols: the scorpion and the ankh, the vital Ancient Egyptian emblem of life. So although it is unlikely that there was an actual ruler called Scorpion, Selket's mythical qualities seem to be associated with whoever the unifier of Egypt was, and the ankh has been held in the hands of successive kings.

RIGHT: **The Larger Scorpion Macehead shows King Narmer with the white crown of Upper Egypt holding a hoe.**

Festivals for gods and the king

Den was an innovator, expansionist and also a supporter of ritual and renewal, in which the gods and their myths shared centre stage. It is in the theatre of ritual and festival that much evidence of gods and their myths is revealed, and described to us in image and writing.

On a small ebony label from an oil jar in his tomb at Abydos, Den is shown taking part in Heb Sed, one of the greatest politico-religious festivals that continued, albeit with changes, through time. Created to celebrate a king's reign, to renew it and to show that the king still had the physical and mental strength to rule, the Heb Sed jubilee required the king's participation on a grand scale, starting with lavish libations in the temples of the gods.

ABOVE: At the Heb Sed festival, the myth of goddess Isis and god Osiris is enacted. Here, Isis protects the golden shrine of Pharaoh Tutankhamun (c. 1333–1323 BCE).

On the right of the label, Den appears running along the festival's ritual course to show his prowess, brandishing the Heb Sed insignia. On the left, he sits enthroned on a raised stage, wearing the crowns of Upper and Lower Egypt. Sed, the jackal-headed god, also known as Wepwawet, and guardian of the route through the underworld, is perhaps also the guardian of the king's challenging festival itinerary, as well as the route through his reign.

Den's reign was long: he succeeded to the throne as a child, and it is believed that his mother, Queen Merneith, acted as regent until he came of age. She was not the first queen to hold such an important position and to represent her own divine status, carrying the name 'Neith', a powerful goddess with a complex mythology.

FIVE ROYAL TITLES

Over time, the kings of Egypt adopted five name types, each associating royalty with the gods.

Horus name – the embodiment of the god Horus in the king, validating his position.

Nebti name – he of the Two Ladies: the vulture goddess Nekhbet of Upper Egypt, and the cobra goddess Wadjet of Lower Egypt.

Golden Horus – Horus featured on top of the symbol for gold, a precious metal representing eternity.

Throne name, or prenomen – a coronation name, eventually trumping Horus. Its main component was Nsw-bty, the 'King of the sut plant (sedge grass of Upper Egypt) and the bee (of Lower Egypt)'. The sun god Re was later incorporated.

Birth name or nomen – often beginning with 'Son of Re', followed by a dynastic name, it reinforced the importance of astrology in theology.

RIGHT: **An eternal golden Horus from the tomb of Pharaoh Tutankhamun (c. 1333–1323 BCE).**

Heb Sed over time

The depictions of the festival during other reigns include running the route with the bull god, Apis, receiving ritual insignia from the Temple of Horus, and being carried down the Nile on a ceremonial boat to represent the sun god Re's successful journey into the underworld. Some kings changed the locations of the events, the gods who were to be honoured, or added reenactments of dramatic myths such as Osiris and Isis's battle with Set and death.

Neith the goddess and Neithotep the queen

Evidence for Ancient Egypt's religious and political mythology was not confined to the serekhs and scenes of kings. There is very little doubt that the first and powerful queen was Neithotep, who carried with her the stories and status of great goddesses. Neithotep's titles are impressive. The first is 'Consort of the Two Ladies' – the 'Two Ladies' referring to Nekhbet and Wadjet, the goddess protectors of a unified Egypt and also the Nebti name for the king of Egypt. The second is 'Foremost of Women'. The name of Queen Neithotep itself means 'Neith is satisfied', and Neith, goddess of both war and weaving, was a deity of great and lasting power. Her roles represent the two ways in which the unification of Upper and Lower Egypt could have occurred. Aggression might have achieved it, though so, too, could the 'weaving' of nation-building.

RIGHT: **The goddess Neith on a tomb mural of Queen Nefertari, wife of Rameses II (1279–1213 BCE)**

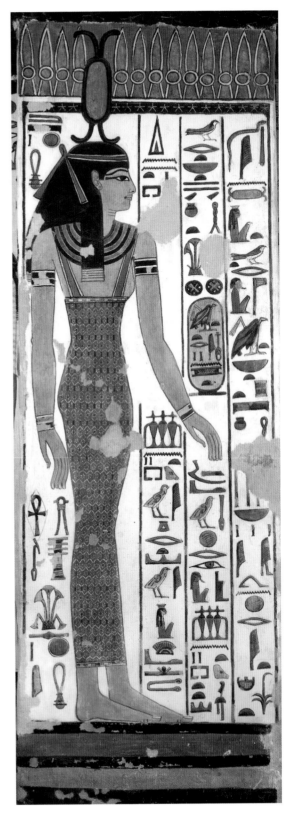

Neith was also the goddess of the red crown of Lower Egypt and of the ancient city of Sais on the Western Delta. She was a creator god; a sky god who fashioned the sun god, Re, with the help of Nun, the god of the primordial soup from which Re arose. Re, the god of hope in the rising sun and the risen dead, was the antithesis of Neith's other creation, Apep, whom she fashioned by spitting into Nun's muddy, swirling waters. Later, Neith's role as the goddess of weaving made her the go-to goddess for reconciliation, especially between Horus and Set, the gods of Upper and Lower Egypt. Her other multifaceted roles became creative rather than destructive, and included moulding the world.

A woman of power

Queen Neithotep's association with this most influential goddess, and the Lower Egypt city of Sais, indicates that she was, or became, a woman of great power and influence in a place of strategic importance. The fact that Neithotep owned her own serekh is indicative of her position. On it, the curved crossed arrows of Neith sit upon Neithotep's enclosed name, mirroring the serekh design of kings. Yet for many Egyptologists, Queen Neithotep's most important role was as wife to the first king of a new Egypt; validating either Narmer or Hor Aha as unifiers and rulers. As Queen Neithotep's tomb contained ivory labels and other artefacts marked with both names in serekhs and symbols, it is hard to know whose consort she was.

However, Queen Neithotep's identity is not questioned, and her tomb was so large that her own high status is a given. Discovered at Naqada in 1897 by Jacques de Morgan, it takes the shape of a mastaba, a precursor of the great pyramids of the Old Kingdom (c. 2686–2160 BCE). Constructed of clay tiles, this mausoleum measured 75 x 184ft (23 x 56m). Inside, the horde of grave goods included copious boxes, cosmetics, figurines and, importantly, those serekhs with symbols for Narmer, Hor Aha and herself, linking her with the kings of unification. The presence of the royal symbols for both would-be unifiers might mean that they were one and the same person. What is certain is that her name and her high-status burial meant that Queen Neithotep was an important member of the new royal family, and so were the goddesses associated with her.

LEFT: A clay jar seal from about 3100 BCE with a central cartouche of Queen Neithotep, found in her mastaba at Naqada.

In mythology, goddesses are powerful not only as lifegivers and protectors but also as malevolent destroyers. Neith was no exception and, through time, reflecting one of her symbols, she wove contrasting threads to create her complex narrative. In history, it is possible that Queen Neithotep was not a mere consort but perhaps a strategist and a diplomat; at the very least, she was one of the powers behind the throne.

Neithotep's massive and well-appointed tomb, with its artefacts and early writing, described the relationship between royalty, gods and myths in a united and powerful Egypt. The tomb was a precursor to pyramids and temples that have become galleries, libraries and museums of the sacred.

2

PYRAMIDS, PALACES, PAPYRUS AND PAINT

The actions and aspects of the gods grew in number and nuance as Egypt evolved into a fully formed theocracy during the Old Kingdom (c. 2686–2160 BCE). The basic skills and tools required to build and run it as a successful nation, from architecture and engineering to paper and pens, were simultaneously used to express and honour the gods and their stories.

Gods, myth and construction

The Old Kingdom marked the beginning of the great pharaonic age, when power and status were manifested in temples, palaces and pyramids. Intrinsic to their design, whether inside or out, were constant references to the gods; royal and divine power were entwined in the very shape of the built environment.

OPPOSITE: In the *Book of the Dead*, Ibis-headed Thoth, god of wisdom and writing, records a deceased's weighing-of-the-heart results.

Under the supervision and blessing of the polymath goddess, Seshat, the kings of Egypt planned their palaces, temples and even their own tombs. Seshat's many skills included measurement and writing, making her instrumental in the eyes of kings and artisans in helping them shape their manmade world. Moreover, she guided them in describing through ink, paint, wood and stone the important roles of gods and their myths within it, and beyond into death.

Up to 11 spiritual and practical ceremonies ensured the safety, beauty and godly approval of each construction, and were

especially important before temple building. It was Seshat who held the king's hand during one of the most important of these ceremonies, the 'Stretching of the Cord', in which the king assisted in driving the stakes holding the cord that marked the perimeter of the building.

With no temples ever dedicated to her, this highly rated goddess of precision, literacy and the keeper of books is shown on temple wall reliefs meticulously recording, for the benefit of the nation, lists of wartime captives and booty. Seshat's solid reputation lasted from at least the Early Dynasties right through to the Ptolemaic period (332–30 BCE), her roles increasing throughout that time.

God and myth in temple foundations

Temple shrines dedicated to gods proliferated throughout Ancient Egypt in the boom years of the Old Kingdom and beyond. Some stood alone as cult temples for individual gods or goddesses, while others were mortuary temples, integrated into the royal complexes of palaces and tombs.

Myth and creation were built into the very structure of a temple, which represented in its stone frame the whole universe. Its alignment along the longitudinal axis symbolized the flow of the sacred Nile. At the core of the traditional temple layout was a design based on the principal creation myth, in which a sky god separated earth and the heavens from a murky soup, and gave Horus, the falcon god of a unified Egypt, an emerging mound of silt on which to perch. In early temples, this mound was often represented by a shaped pile of sand.

Over time, a national symbolism of gods and their myths developed. This was expressed in temple interiors through wall

BELOW: **The great god Amun's central building was part of Karnak Temple Complex, with its temples, pylons, statues and chapels.**

ABOVE: **At Karnak, rituals to the sun god, Amun, were depicted on Amenhotep IV's temple walls in a talatat construction, i.e. made of 283 small sandstone blocks.**

paintings, statues, vessels and figurines, from small shrines to the greatest temple complex at Karnak, dedicated to the ram-headed god, Amun.

Amun, an ancient creation deity, whose name, image and symbolism changed over time and whose status rose to the highest rank, began as a quiet Theban cult god of air and fertility. Then, when Thebes was made capital of Egypt during parts of the Middle Kingdom (c. 2055–1650 BCE) and the New Kingdom (c. 1550–1069 BCE), he was plucked from relative obscurity and rose to the position of a state god, later melded with the sun god Re, until the end of the kingdom of Egypt in 30 CE. Amun's mystical, mercurial nature enabled him to become the god of many things – whatever suited the needs of any particular time period and ruler. His story is a good example of the way in which his biographical trajectory and his varied fortunes are reflected in changes to the design, size and condition of cult temples generally.

Early cult temples, open to the air, were accessed through a hall facing the mysterious desert, a place of chaos that only a god could calm. A pyramidal obelisk, a benben, was the focus of devotion within the main space, and an altar stood for the priest to present ritual offerings and libations to the god or goddess. Rooms for storing food and votive objects with which to honour the gods surrounded the central sanctuary.

In time, temple sanctuaries became spaces for rituals and dramas performed by the priesthood and from where festival parades could begin. During these festivals, the statue, which replaced the benben, was ceremoniously removed by the priests and paraded along a specific route. In Amun's case, an arena was constructed for solar rituals involving his creation myth, which developed into one of Ancient Egypt's most spectacular pageants.

In contrast to early temples, Karnak, a labyrinthine complex of great stone pylons that separated enormous halls, is breathtaking but haphazard in its design, reflecting the fortunes of the kings who were associated with Amun through the ages. Built from about 2055 BCE, Karnak endured through times of royal strife, when it was rather neglected. In times of royal resurgence, such as during the New Kingdom (1550–1069 BCE), Karnak entered a renaissance, expanding to include the family of Amun. Fresh pylons were constructed, accessing new temples to the lioness-headed goddess Mut, the mother figure for the nation and Amun's wife, and Khonsu, their son, the moon god. A courtyard for Montu, a god of war, reflected his importance as a newly appointed aspect of Amun.

KARNAK'S GREAT HYPOSTYLE HALL AND MYTH

Karnak temple's impressive hypostyle hall, an area where the roof is supported by pylons, measures nearly 5000sq m (54,000sq ft) and is lined with 134 stone columns. A temple's hypostyle hall was a grand central space designed to represent marshland at the beginning of time, when the gods separated earth from sky. The tall stone columns arose from it as papyrus reeds, and small roof lights allowed sunbeams to shine along the central rib of the hall's floor, throwing chinks of light on the darkness and chaos of the emerging world.

RIGHT: **Sculpted pillars of the Hypostyle Hall are part of the Karnak Temple, known as *Ipt-Swt*, 'The Most Select of Places'.**

Temples of theatre

The temple festivals for Amun, Mut and Khonsu became celebrations of the order that comes out of the unity of a relationship made in heaven. They played out the Ma'at myth in which calm and cooperation must always overcome chaos. Beginning from the Middle Kingdom (2055–1650 BCE), one of the greatest of these spectacles was the Festival of Opet, a 20-day ceremony that took place at Karnak.

Every year after harvest, when the soil and the gods were exhausted, nature and the heavens were left vulnerable to the forces of evil. The festival aimed to restore the equilibrium of Ma'at and rejuvenate both gods and the king. It reinforced the relationship between the divine king of the earth with Amun, the creator god of heaven, and of Amun's relationship with Mut, his wife. Amun's statue, believed to be the embodiment of the god himself, was carried in a ceremonial barque that floated on the great temple lake at Karnak, from which it was transported to the temple complex at Luxor. Temple architecture grew to include festival space, and in this case the lake was created specifically for the Festival of Opet.

BELOW: Priests carry the great god Amun's likeness in a temple procession, accompanied by dancers and heralded by trumpeters.

The massive stonework of the temple itself symbolized the eternity of Amun, who became the greatest of the creator gods, his mercurial nature absorbing many changes through time. Inside, images, script and statuary tell us the stories of Amun and his family, who became known as the Triad. Together, the components of the complex have become narrators of their power and myths.

Temples for the kings

The kings' role in temple life was vital to the continuity of the gods' divine story enshrined within. It was the kings' job to build and maintain temple structures throughout the land, in fear of the gods, to perpetuate and augment their narratives, and because their reputations depended on their show of dedication. In turn, the gods took care of the country and the king, guarding his journey through the afterlife, a mythical journey mapped out in tombs, especially the great pyramids.

Temples linked to these pyramids are known as mortuary temples, where food and objects could be offered to the 'ka', or spirit, of the king in his afterlife, rather than to a god or goddess. As such, mortuary temples are distinguished from cult temples, though as cults flourished for divine kings themselves, the distinction between them is perhaps rather slim. What is certain is that, as with a cult temple, the nature of gods and their myths were incorporated into the design and decoration of the pyramid complex, including mortuary temples attached to it.

RAMESES III, POWER AND AMUN

Like Rameses II, Rameses III (1187–1156 BCE) honoured Amun by expanding the Karnak complex. Inside the temple, a small pylon depicts Rameses striking his foe outside a chapel complex for ceremonial barques. The first courtyard is lined with two rows of Osiride statues: pillars shaped as a mummy-like body with fists clenched and arms crossed over the chest. These statues show the king wearing the southern red crown on the west side and the white crown of the north on the east. The second hypostyle hall leads to three shrines for the ritual Karnak barques of Amun.

ABOVE: **Rameses III defended Egypt from two Libyan invasions. On this wall painting he returns triumphantly from a campaign.**

ABOVE: Pillars topped with capitals representing goddess Hathor once supported the ceiling of this temple at Elephantine.

Myth in the plan of the pyramid complex

Gods and their narratives were embodied in nature and natural forces, which dictated the choice of a pyramid's site and aspect. Deities are apparent in the very geography of Egypt: in its topography, drainage system and its position under the stars at auspicious times of the year; in specific deserts and oases, mountains and gullies; and in the valley of the great River Nile, the source of plenty and the Kingdom of Egypt itself.

Temple foundations and the sun's cycle

At Giza, the Great Pyramid of Khufu and the Khafre pyramid, and at Dahshur, the Red Pyramid, are almost perfectly aligned with the cardinal points, and the structures along which the king's body was ceremonially carried ran from east to west. Beginning with the valley temple at the sacred Nile's edge in the

ANUKET, GODDESS OF THE CATARACTS

The goddess Anuket was one of the water deities that guarded the spectacular cataracts from which water cascaded during the Nile's inundation. Ancient Egyptians believed that the cataracts marked the source of the Nile, so its protection was vital. Originally a deity from Nubia, south of Egypt, she was depicted wearing a crown of Nile reeds and ostrich feathers.

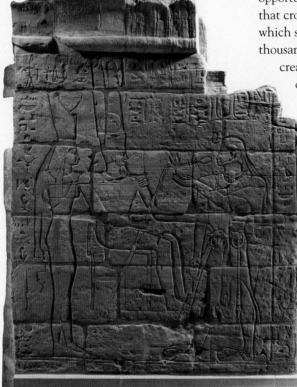

Pyramids were sited in the desert to the west of the Nile. On the riverbank to the east rose temples that served the main pyramid complexes. These temples were an important ceremonial point on the king's journey before entombment in the pyramid, which was built well away from the threat of flooding.

The desert of the west was the face of hardship and chaos, yet also a route to opportunity via the web of perilous trade routes that crossed it. It was the mysterious land from which so many Ancient Egyptians had come, thousands of years before the kingdom was created. More than this, it was the place of the setting sun and therefore, too, of the sun god Re's daily journey into the darkness of death. As such, the west was an important cardinal point in calculating the most auspicious orientation of a particular structure.

The sun, moon and stars had steered the traveller across the desert for millennia; for Ancient Egyptians, the cosmology was a guiding force in navigating this life and the next. Its power and importance dictated the orientation of royal building projects, from palaces to pyramids.

east, a canal and covered causeway led to the walled pyramid complex in the west, where the body of the king was received.

Here, the setting sun, 'dying' over the stark desert, represented the start of the pharaoh's journey with the sun god Re towards his resurrection as Osiris, god of the afterlife. A pyramid's point was thought to symbolize the sun, personified by Re, while the sun's beams were represented by the pyramid's angled sides and sharp edges that spread out towards earth at its base.

ABOVE: **Anuket's power spread afar. Here, Nubia's Kushite King Aspelta (c. 600–580 BCE) makes offerings to Anuket and Amun-Re.**

The equinox and the pyramids

In 2014, American engineer and archaeologist Glen Dash proposed that Ancient Egypt's architects were able to align the pyramid with the cardinal points by setting the aspect of its foundations on 22 September, the autumn equinox. At this time, day and night are equal due to the earth's tilt being halfway between the summer and winter solstices. Dash worked out that a surveyor could fix a rod perpendicular to the ground and plot the sun's shadow throughout the day, resulting in a line running almost perfectly from east to west, and thus finding true north.

By the time of pyramid building, kings had become pharaohs, a title that means 'great house'. Djoser (2667–2648 BCE), the first pharaoh to construct a pyramid, began with a comparably modest flat-topped mastaba. He erected it at Saqqara, a new necropolis site that he had designated near Memphis, which was Egypt's capital at this time.

Imhotep, a divine architect

Djoser's mastaba was not grand enough, so, taking advantage of a boom in the economy and especially an increase in agricultural production, he invested in a much larger, more iconic tomb. Yet even with all this wealth, his plan would have been fanciful had it not been for Imhotep, the pharaoh's vizier and also a physician, sage, astrologer, master scribe and architect.

That we separate these disciplines is perhaps a modern-day misunderstanding of Ancient Egypt's approach to problem-solving. Using these skills together, Imhotep was able to design a complex that reflected the forces of the gods, their mythical deeds and the pharaoh's everlasting power. These principles led to the construction of the first pyramid made from cut stone blocks. Its robust material and building method reflect strength and longevity, while the steps that make it an amazingly tall building for its time also have meaning, it is thought, as a stairway to the sun god, Re.

Imhotep, whose name means 'one who comes in peace', had served not only the king and the gods but also the people. Unusually, a hundred years after his death he was rewarded for his intelligence and devotion by being declared a demigod, although it took until the Persian conquest in 525 BCE for him to be called a god proper.

So great was Imhotep's status that, in the Triad of great Memphis deities, he replaced Nefertem, a mercurial young god who was at once a serene blue lotus that had emerged from the

OPPOSITE: **Khufu and Khafre pyramids here, and the Red Pyramid, are only one fifteenth of one degree out of alignment with the cardinal points.**

swamp at the dawn of time and a confrontational warring lion. His parents, Ptah, creator of the universe, and Sekhmet, the goddess of war and disease, were the other two deities in the Triad. Replacing their son was a huge promotion for Imhotep. It is possible that his qualities as a healer helped to reconcile the two seemingly opposing forces of Ptah and Sekhmet, so maintaining equilibrium, or Ma'at, in the heavens.

The Djoser step pyramid is the god Imhotep's visible legacy, but it was his services to medicine and healing that led to his place in the pantheon. As with other belief systems that followed, his saintly deeds became enlarged in myth. Over centuries, his followers brought clay models of diseased body parts and mummified ibises to the Saqqara necropolis, to temples that he had built in Memphis, and to the banks of the sacred Nile, in the hopes of being cured of their ailments. The Djoser pyramid, while embodying Djoser and the gods, also represents the god Imhotep, and his deeds that were transformed into miracles and myth.

Myth in the landscape: the mountain of Anubis

A pyramid-shaped mountain rises above low desert to the west of the Nile, obscuring the range behind it and so appearing as if it stands alone, like a manmade royal tomb. During the Middle Kingdom (2055–1650 BCE), the sacred site of Mount Anubis was cleverly chosen by the pharaoh Senusret III (1875–1855 BCE) as an auspicious setting for a burial complex deep underground. High on the cliffs, Anubis, the jackal-headed god of the desert and guardian of the mountain, protects the site. Moreover, as his name means 'decay', Anubis oversees the embalming of Senusret's body before accompanying him through the perilous underworld; simultaneously, as 'jackal of the nine bows', he guards the pharaoh against his enemies in the darkness.

LEFT: **This Old Kingdom bronze statue shows wise Imhotep, who some scholars link with the Biblical figure, Joseph.**

ANUBIS THE HEALER

In myth, Anubis, like Ma'at, creates harmony and wholeness out of chaos and disintegration. As the son of Osiris and Nephthys, he was high in the pantheon rankings. It was he who helped Isis to put Osiris's body back together after vengeful Set had dismembered it, cutting it into 13 pieces. Anubis embalmed the body, apart from one piece, making it ready and whole for Isis to resurrect Osiris using her sorcery.

The tomb at the foot of the Mountain of Anubis is seen as a trendsetter in royal burials: a precursor to the New Kingdom's vast royal burial site, the Valley of the Kings, also on the west bank of the Nile, near Luxor. Both locations showed a new preference for letting the gods' natural features become shrines for kings rather than less impressive manmade alternatives. Crucially, pyramids were also seen as more vulnerable to tomb raiders, although this proved unfounded.

Senusret III's name means 'Man of Useret', a goddess associated with power, and sometimes represented with a bow and arrow, yet rarely cited in myth. Her reticence was not mirrored in Senusret, who, as an epic builder of eight great fortresses, had already constructed an impressive brick pyramid complex faced with limestone at Dahshur, just south of Memphis and where other pyramids rise. A granite sarcophagus was discovered there in 1894, but Senusret did not end up in it. He had turned his back on it to excavate a site set in a landscape matched in its sacredness by the nearby city necropolis of South Abydos, which was dedicated to Osiris, god of the underworld.

Although based in Memphis, Senusret III had become devoted to Osiris, so Abydos seems to have been a very conscious choice. His complex, a marvel of engineering, is set 30m (100ft) below the level of the desert, with an elaborate route of interconnected corridors and chambers plunging a further 80m (260ft).

ABOVE: **Rameses I, who was probably from a miltary family, faces stern Anubis on a tomb painting in the Valley of the Kings.**

It is lined with limestone and red quartzite, with double walls between which were hidden Senusret's sarcophagus and canopic chest. After building it, the access corridor to the royal burial chamber was blocked with massive hewn chunks of granite – although not even this stopped the tomb raiders.

Despite constructing more than one lavish and elaborate burial complex, Senusret's body has not yet been found, although the pyramid site at Dahshur is generously filled with royal women and high officials. Archaeologists are hoping that he will be found beneath the Mountain of Anubis, although Anubis seems to be protecting it rather well.

Senusret's burial complex, set in a sacred landscape,
enables the deceased's journey to follow the inner geological
undulations of the site itself. As such, some Egyptologists
describe Senusret's creation as the first 'Amduat tomb'.
Amduat, the 'Book of the Hidden Chamber', is the most
important 'Book of the Netherworld', and narrates the sun
god Re's topographical journey from west to east over the
underworld's terrain.

First scripted and illustrated on royal tombs in the
Eighteenth–Twentieth Dynasties during the New Kingdom
(1550–1069 BCE), long after Senusret's death, the Amduat was
later published on papyrus, mostly as fragmented text. It is
thought that some architectural features in Senusret's complex
follow the journey described in the text; text and architecture
perhaps coincide in the central burial chamber where, at the
central point of the Amduat journey, the pharaoh will be as one
with Osiris and Re. Perhaps, also, the lined vertical shaft of the
complex allows a comforting light to shine on Osiris in the
dark night of the Duat, the realm of the dead.

The Mountain of Anubis and the Valley of the Kings were
colossal expressions and evidence of the power of gods and
their narratives in nature. But whether natural or manmade,
visible or hidden, all royal burial complexes were packed with
artworks, artefacts and scripts that described the roles and
natures of the gods.

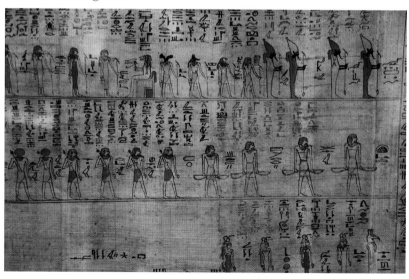

Myths in models

Well before pyramids and rock tombs, from at least about 4500 BCE, the gods and their strengths in myth were modelled in clay, carved in wood or shaped in stone. Especially popular were amulets, worn by rich and poor alike. For the rich, these representations of godly powers of protection were fashioned in expensive materials such as gold, even more precious silver, and colourful stones such as lapis lazuli. For the poor, they were often moulded from faience, an aggregate made from crushed sand or stone, which self-glazed when finished.

The power of the amulet cannot be understated; it was seen as capable of protecting the wearer from any danger or tricky situation, in life or in death. Just as there was a god or goddess for anything and everything, so there was an amulet that represented a deity or an aspect of their power, character or myth. Its potency was only released after a professional amulet expert had performed an 'opening' ritual on it.

BELOW: **The blue-green of this wedjat eye amulet from the Third Intermediate Period shows the healing of Horus's torn eye.**

COLOUR IN MYTH

Paint pigments were used as a language to represent gods' characteristics or roles in myth.

Real gold, and golden-yellow pigment, represented the gods' flesh, especially the sun god, Re. The pigment was made from orpiment, a sulphide of arsenic. Gold, like the gods, never tarnished.

Silver was a most precious metal to Ancient Egyptians as it was hard to obtain. As such it represented the bones of the gods.

Blue-green, made from ground malachite or from copper, stood for protection; renewal and fertility, rebirth and resurrection. As such it was the colour of Hathor, Osiris, and the skin of Nephthys.

Red, from red ochre, iron oxide or realgar (a disulphide of arsenic), coloured men's skin and represented many opposing qualities, from life force to evil, like the god, Set.

Black, from charcoal or soot, represented the underworld, and Osiris in his darkness. It also symbolized Kemet, the land of the black Nile silt.

An amulet expert also acted as an ongoing consultant, recommending a whole suite of personalized amulets for any given individual and situation. He performed spells or recitations over an amulet when a client was in difficulty, referring to myths of gods who had the power through their stories to bring triumph or success to the amulet's wearer. Papyrus records mention that spells were performed over amulets in the afterlife to protect the deceased against the perils of the underworld, and they were tucked into the bandages of the mummified body to help it on its way.

As the predynastic period ended and the kingdom of Egypt truly began, wealth grew and trade expanded, so that new materials and art techniques made the high-status amulet a thing of beauty and often of colour. Like all things, colour imbued extra meaning into the amulet, which never lost its potency through the ages.

ABOVE: Ptolemy V (205–180 BCE) honours Buchis, the bull incarnation of war god, Montu. The gold highlights Buchis's sacredness.

Every picture tells a story

Colour in art is part of the language used to express myths and the natures of gods and goddesses on temple, palace and pyramid walls; on stele and sarcophagi. Ancient Egyptians understood well the deep meaning and history of rich images that combined gods in human form or as anthropomorphized animal deities, colours that reflected their natures, and symbols associated with their guardianship roles and myth narratives.

When symbols transformed into hieroglyphs, the stories of the gods perhaps spoke in a less immediate and nuanced way. This is possibly one reason why text was often interspersed with images of the gods, whose symbolism changed as gods' roles developed and became more complex through the dynasties. Yet text, based on symbols, became indispensable to pharaohs in areas other

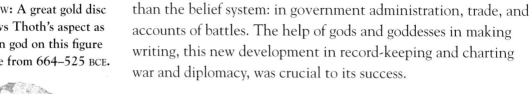

BELOW: **A great gold disc shows Thoth's aspect as moon god on this figure made from 664–525 BCE.**

than the belief system: in government administration, trade, and accounts of battles. The help of gods and goddesses in making writing, this new development in record-keeping and charting war and diplomacy, was crucial to its success.

Thoth, god of writing, calculation and the moon

The mathematical genius of the goddess Seshat, who assisted the gods in construction and record-keeping, was matched by her husband, Thoth, a god with the elegant head of an ibis. Using his mastery of calculation, Thoth was able to navigate the moon safely through the night sky and collate its movements into a year, dividing it into months. Therefore, as controller of time, and as the supreme god of all scribes, he also became the writer of history, which we call myth.

It was Thoth who used hieroglyphs and made them into objects, creating anything he desired. He conjured thoughts that came from the heart and soul of the sun god, Re, and was the tongue of Ptah, the god who fashioned the whole universe. With such expression at his fingertips, Thoth was able to write spells to help humans through their trials in this life and the next, with formulae for everything, including emotions such as love, and cures for seemingly incurable pain. It was he who dulled the sting from the scorpion that struck Horus when he was young and later brought sight to the eye that Set had ripped from his head.

Through the position of Thoth in the pantheon, it is clear that Ancient Egyptians revered the power of the written word, though for many centuries it was not a power possessed by ordinary people. 'Hier' itself means 'sacred' in Greek, expressing the reverence for writing, and the idea that, like the gods, it was everlasting.

The key to the written myths

If not for the Napoleonic Wars, hieroglyphs and the mythical gods they helped to describe would have remained a mystery far longer than they did. For Napoleon Bonaparte, as well as being an imperialist, saw himself as a man of letters. So, during the Egyptian campaign between 1798 and 1801, while attempting to sever Britain's access through the Red Sea to its lucrative eastern commercial interests in India and beyond, Napoleon sent a clutch of academics to Egypt. Their purpose was to unlock its secrets, and the party included architects, scientists, economists and a broad range of artists.

One of the party, engineer François-Xavier Bouchard, discovered a large slab of inscribed grey-green granite embedded in a fortress wall in Rosetta, a town on the Nile near Alexandria. On it were three separate sets of scripts: hieroglyphic, demotic and Greek. It was clearly a document of distinction, destined for analysis in France. Disappointingly for Napoleon, he was defeated by Britain at the Battle of Alexandria on 21 March 1801. The victorious troops were instructed to requisition all artefacts found by the French, and cart them off home.

Before this, the French had judiciously made copies of the Rosetta Stone's scripts. In 1822, classicist Jean-François Champollion (1790–1832), thinking that the texts all imparted the same information, cracked the code of the hieroglyphs using the one language he did know: Greek. He began by identifying the name Ptolemy V in Greek, then matched it with a royal

BELOW: Napoleon I rides up to a half-buried sphinx in this engraving, from J.L. Gerome's painting.

BELOW: The Rosetta Stone was engraved with a decree on the instruction of King Ptolemy V at Memphis in about 196 BCE.

cartouche that stood out similarly in the hieroglyph section of text. This was the start of unravelling the written language of the Egyptians, which unlocked one of the most expansive pantheons and mythologies in the world. From this we now know much of the content of religious texts and references throughout the ages.

SCRIPTS THROUGH TIME

Hieroglyphs were combinations of pictograms (pictorial representations of words or phrases), ideograms (signs or characters representing an idea without indicating what the word sounds like), logograms (signs or characters representing a word or phrase) and phonograms (where a picture represents a sound as well as itself) showing gods, people, physical objects and sounds. The earliest piece of evidence of hieroglyphs so far stretches back to about 4500 BCE, on an ivory seal from Nubt, an urban centre in Upper Egypt that faces the gold sources of the eastern desert. Hieroglyphs were the privilege of royalty, priests and the upper classes and were used in temples and tombs.

ABOVE: **Hieroglyph in Greek means 'sacred carving'.**

Hieratic script developed around 3150 BCE, from the beginning of Egypt's unification. It was used to create a more nuanced language, emphasizing the use of phonograms and logograms. In this way, abstract ideas, feelings, colours and movement could be expressed. These were joined together in a fast and free-flowing language. As such, it was perfect for administrative as well as religious purposes, and for the well-to-do, becoming a more democratized script for the religious needs of the middle classes.

Demotic script emerged as an even faster form of writing based on hieratic script. It was developed in the seventh century BCE under Psamtik I (664–610 BCE). It was used until the fifth century CE and was the script of commerce and administration, leaving hieratic script to express the belief system.

ABOVE: **Demotic in Greek means 'of ordinary folk'.**

Coptic script developed with the rise of Christianity under the Greeks, the new rulers of Egypt from 330 BCE. They eschewed Egyptian script apart from six demotic symbols, which they incorporated into their own alphabet.

ABOVE: **Coptic is the last Ancient Egyptians language.**

ABOVE: **This clear script, created in relief, is taken from the Pyramid Text of Admiral Tjanhebu at Saqqara from 664– 525 BCE.**

Pyramid Texts: a path for the royal dead

Pyramid Texts were the first written narratives of the higher gods and goddesses, although they were partial and laid out only in a quasi-organized way. Their purpose was not to tell a story but to guide a dead king's soul, a complex conglomerate of about eight most sacred spiritual components, to an eternal and blissful afterlife.

This could only be achieved through spells and the judgement or protection of the gods, depending on which stage of the journey he was at. Moreover, deities were there to ensure that the king's body remained intact and, reunited with the soul, whole and immortal; not just like a god but as one. Before this happy time, the king's journey would take his preserved body up steps, ladders, ramps and through periods of flight, challenged by evil and saved by his strength in the face of it, and the grace of the gods.

From about 2350 BCE, during the Fifth and Sixth Dynasties, Pyramid Texts appeared as funerary wall inscriptions on pyramids.

They were based on more ancient oral traditions and were fragmentary. This is perhaps partly why the texts are known as utterances, although that might also refer to priests reading or chanting them aloud.

The script is haphazard and inconsistent. There are gaps in the narrative and some hieroglyphs are obscure and incomplete, suggesting perhaps a deliberate attempt to confuse evil forces that might thwart the king's eternal happiness. On the other hand, it might just be that the spells, gods and mythical allusions were so well known as oral incantations that it was not necessary to be exact or explicit.

Through these texts, and in later versions through illustrations, we are informed in some detail about the elaborate processes involved in preparing the corpse for the afterlife; these processes were rich in mythical significance.

Myth in mummification

Anubis, jackal-headed protector of the dead, Lord of the Sacred Lands of the necropoli and god of embalming, had supervised the preservation of the god Osiris after Set's murderous attack on his brother. In honour of Anubis's skills and power, *sem* priests, whose sole function was to perform mortuary rituals on deceased kings or their statues, often wore jackal-headed masks and spotted skins over their white clothes in preparation for the task ahead.

Strengthened and instructed by Anubis and their other patron gods – the great Osiris and Ptah, and Sokar,

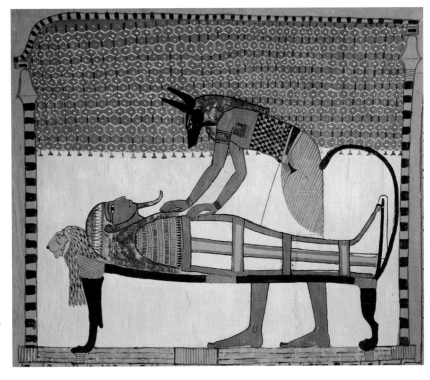

BELOW: As god of embalming, Anubis stands over the deceased. He was also Keeper of the Scales, for weighing the heart.

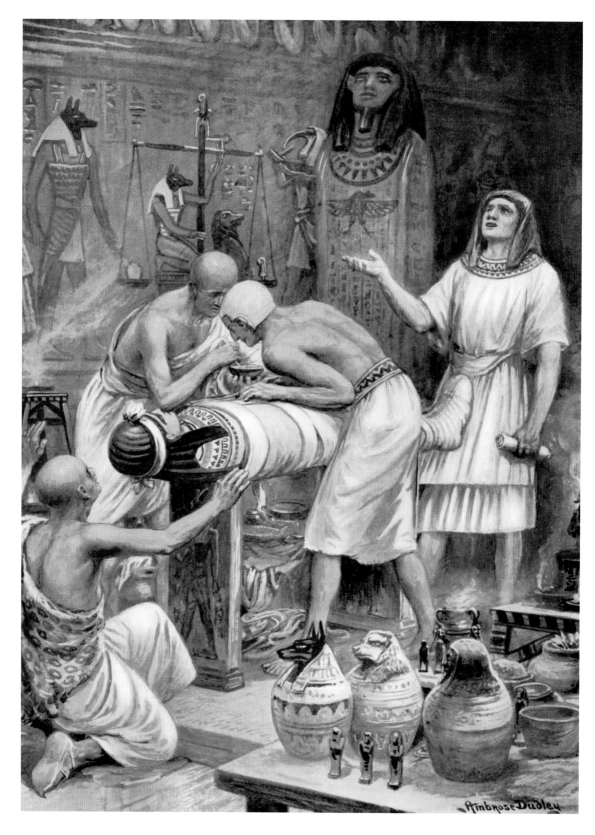

the Memphis god of necropoli – the priests, standing in for the eldest son of the king if he was unable, performed the mummification. Using bespoke tools, mineral salts and perfumed resins, they performed the lengthy procedure. This involved evisceration and dehydration to chemical preservation and the all-important predynastic 'Opening of the Mouth' ceremony, in up to 75 'episodes', which by the Old Kingdom included the eyes, nose and ears.

These apertures not only allowed the mummified body to eat, drink, see, smell and hear on the journey through the underworld but also released the part of the very complex soul that was associated with the body, and allowed all a person's spirit forms to play their part in the eventual reunification of the whole person.

Kings and gods in times of change

Did the king, now whole and in a heavenly parallel but perfect world, emerge as Osiris, god of the moon and the dark night? Or was he transformed into Re, god of the radiant sun? The preferences of kings for different gods through time were played out in the Pyramid Texts and on wall paintings, as one or other high god became the highest of all. Writings and paintings on tomb walls reflected not only the dynamics of individual kings and dynasties but also the ongoing power play between kings and nomarchs, whose totemic gods and their narratives rose and fell as the political landscape changed. Promotion and demotion was felt from time to time, too, by the gods of Egypt's shifting capital cities: Osiris of Abydos, Ptah of Memphis, and Re of Heliopolis who, when fused with Amun of Hermopolis, became the greatest and most enduring god of all. Yet for all its

A COMPLEX SOUL

An Ancient Egyptian's mysterious concept of a soul work together with Kha, a tangible body made eternal only through preservation and mummification.

Ka – a twin of the Kha form that hovers around it, free to move within and without a body and manmade likenesses of it, and able to eat and drink.

Ren – a person's true but secret and mystical name, hidden from others lest they destroy it, and therefore the person, or adopt it for nefarious means.

Ab – the heart, and a person's source of good and evil. It can live forever in the heavens or be devoured by Amut; Ma'at's judgement will prevail.

Ba – a human-headed bird that feeds and gives breath to the deceased during the day. At night, Ba accompanies Re on his heavenly solar barque.

Khaibita – a body's shadow that always hovers near Ba, which can nourish itself with food offerings in the tomb.

Sahu – the spiritual and mental core and deep intentions of a person that remains with them after judgement by Ma'at, for good or for evil.

Akhu – the radiant life force that shines within Sahu and lives on in the heavens.

Sekhem – the motor-like spiritual power within a person that joins Akhu in the heavens.

OPPOSITE: **This painting by Ambrose Dudley (1867–1951) shows mortuary priests working hard to embalm the body.**

ABOVE: **King Unas's burial chamber walls sported the first Pyramid Texts, incised and painted blue. Stars cover the sarcophagus chamber ceiling.**

seeming importance, this dialogue between kings and gods was lost on most Ancient Egyptians, who just wanted the right to die knowing that they would live again somewhere else, just like kings and, increasingly, noblemen.

Myths and magic for the masses

Although Ancient Egyptians of all classes saw gods and their myths in everything, they were denied access to spells and rituals that ensured their eternity and oneness with a higher god. It is not hard to imagine the disappointment and anxiety of those who could afford a downscaled version of the sacred texts but had none to buy.

But towards the end of the Old Kingdom (2686–2160 BCE), mortuary priests, favoured by pharaohs and exempted from taxes, became increasingly wealthy, independent and unruly. So did nomarchs from the regions, who began to pull away from the

MANY ROADS TO HELL

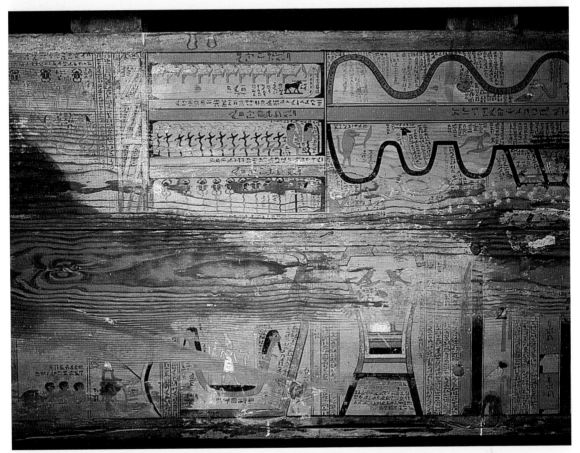

ABOVE: **Coffin Texts cover a coffin floor of Gua, chief physician of Djehutyhotep, governor of Bersha.**

The journey into the afterlife was not for the faint-hearted: failure to set out on it, or to flunk the ordeals the deceased faced, were met with painful punishments, as set out in a number of texts.

The Book of Amduat or **the Book of the Hidden Room** (1552–1306 BCE). Two registers of this book give two different but equally perilous fates for those destined for hell. In register three, the damned are removed from the group of the deceased and refused permission to carry on along the River of Duat towards immortality.

The Book of Gates (1315–1201 BCE) and the **Book of the Earth** (1213–1152 BCE) are grim catalogues of torture inflicted on a deceased sinner condemned to the darkness of hell; they are tied up, often beheaded, then dismembered and burned, making it impossible for the person to rise from death with Re, the morning sun.

The **Book of Caverns** (1186–1069) – for the first time, women suffer the same fate as men. Both are depicted in various extreme and painful positions, beheaded and with their hearts gouged out.

control at the capital, Memphis. The Old Kingdom began to collapse, its finances in a dire state owing to pharaohs' excessive building programmes, especially their lavish pyramids. The old order was crumbling.

There followed a period of decentralization called the First Intermediate Period (2160–2055 BCE), during which Egypt as a nation was, for a while, fragmented and rudderless. But Egypt as a patchwork of independent and quite wealthy nomes was an opportunity for the burgeoning middle classes to enjoy many of the things previously denied them. They acquired high-status, beautifully crafted goods in expensive materials: gold, garnet, carnelian or lapis lazuli. More than this, they were able to afford immortality, and there was no oppressive pharaoh around to stop them.

On their coffins, now not only of wood but also of ceramic or stone, scribes and craftspeople painted mythical spells, rituals, incantations and guide maps for the dead, leading the middle-class deceased soul to the same oneness with a higher god as the nobility. They were finally granted equal access to gods and goddesses who, through their mythical powers, might help them through the ordeals in the underworld that they would face or, conversely, condemn them to perpetual darkness. At least now the masses had a chance.

Coffin Texts

Coffin Texts were at first accessible to noblemen and officials of high rank, filtering down in time to the other classes, and used until the end of the Middle Kingdom in about 1650 BCE. They were derived from the Pyramid Texts and covered about 1185 spells, incantations and formulae. Although not as extensive as the Pyramid Texts, the powers of the gods within them were just as potent, and the chances of the deceased's soul reaching a blissful afterlife just as great as those of a king or queen.

The texts were written in hieratic script, which was normally used for accounts and transactions or administrative correspondence, and associated more with clerks than kings. This is what helped the texts to become more accessible to a wide spectrum of society, as the more rarified hieroglyph writer

RIGHT: **This Coffin Text detail was taken from the coffin of Nespawershepi, chief scribe at the Temple of Amun around 984 BCE.**

COFFIN TEXT SPELL 74, FOR THE REVIVAL OF OSIRIS

While the myths of many gods and goddesses were told in the Coffin Texts, it was the story of the risen Osiris that most people identified with, hoping that they too would be resurrected and be at one with him. Here, Isis and Nephthys reawaken their brother.

> *Ah Helpless One!*
> *Ah Helpless One Asleep!*
> *Ah Helpless One in this place*
> *which you know not; yet I know it!*
> *Behold, I have found you*
> *lying on your side*
> *the great Listless One.*
> *'Ah, Sister!' says Isis to Nephthys,*
> *'This is our brother.*
> *Come let us lift up his head.*
> *Come, let us reassemble his limbs*
> *Come let us put an end*
> *to all his woe, that, as far as*
> *we can help, he will weary*
> *no more.*
>
> (Lewis Spence)

Crucially, the Coffin Texts included the Book of the Two Ways, which was not a book as we know it but a vital set of detailed maps – a kind of cosmographical guide illustrated on the floor of the coffin. Discovered first in the Barsha necropolis in Middle Egypt and dating back to at least the Middle Kingdom (2055–1650) BCE, the maps guide the deceased along one of two winding ways to the heavenly Field of Offerings, where they will meet with Osiris and feast with him.

Like all others in the afterlife, the journey is a set of trials and tests, as the deceased faces perilous demons, mountainous stone walls and the Lake of Fire, which separates the two paths that lead to Rostau, the land of Osiris. It is here that Osiris's body lies, between the inferno and the darkness of the night sky, the domain of the sky god Nut. Any exhausted soul who manages to look upon the body of Osiris has triumphed, and will live forever.

The Coffin Texts were the saviour for many Ancient Egyptians, and were used until the end of the Middle Kingdom in 1650 BCE, when a complete revolution occurred, opening up access to the afterlife.

was not required. The texts were also written in the first person and as such were a direct communication with the spiritual world, without reference to any hierarchy.

The *Book of the Dead* – a chance for the masses

The importance of the Coffin Texts to the masses cannot be overstated: together with the Pyramid Texts, they formed the content of the *Book of the Dead*, which, from the New Kingdom (1550–1069 BCE), really democratized access to the afterlife to all but the poorest.

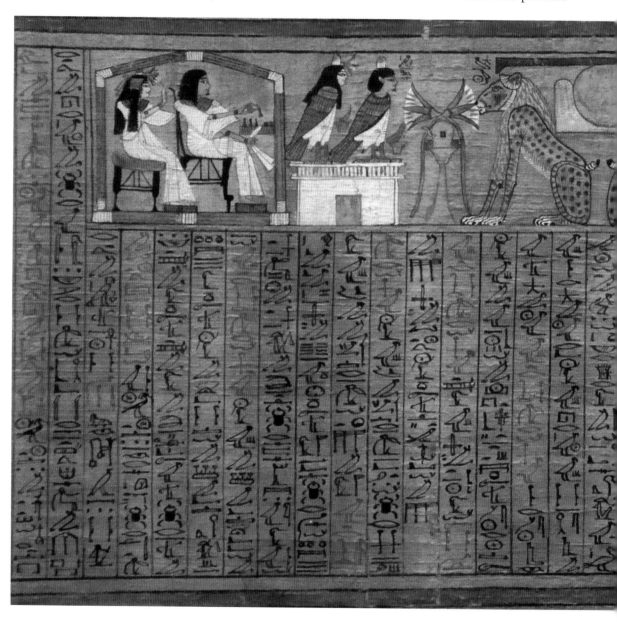

Known also as *The Book of Coming Forth by Day* or *Spells for Going Forth by Day*, they became commercialized texts written quickly by an enormous body of professional scribes, mostly in black ink and on the very portable material of papyrus paper. No two copies were exactly alike; these were more like bespoke prescriptions, guiding an individual's soul as the rather aggressive Divine Ferryman rowed it across the Lake of Lilies and on to the Field of Reeds.

The power of the gods to help or hinder the soul could be precised on papyrus and tucked into tombs and graves in the

BELOW: This *Book of the Dead* text from the 1250 BCE *Papyrus of Ani* shows the ba spirits of Ani, a scribe, and his wife.

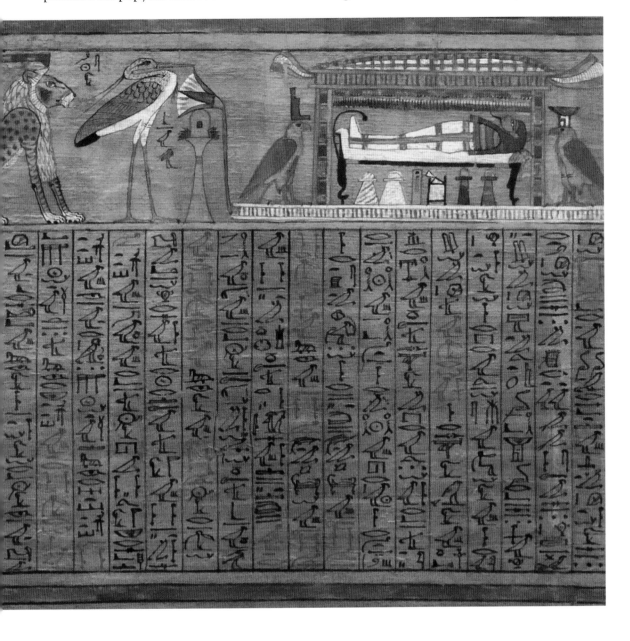

OPPOSITE: **Ma'at,** goddess of truth and balance, was also one of harmony, keeping peace between the world of the living and the dead.

ground. More than just a manual, the spells and codes within the *Book of the Dead* enabled the deceased's spirit parts to transform into mythical creatures whose powers enabled the soul to progress through the afterlife and be at one with a great god.

Gods of grace and gods of wrath

During the journey of the deceased, the roles of gods and goddesses amply reflected their characteristics, which were made apparent in myths with which the Ancient Egyptians were very familiar. So in spells such as 125 of the *Book of the Dead*, the actions of the deities, whether cruel or kind, would not have been unexpected.

In Spell 125, jackal-headed Anubis guides the deceased to the Hall of Truth, where Osiris is ready to judge the heart. The deceased declares his or her moral fitness to proceed on their journey, pleading honesty as they try to assure those present that they did not commit 42 named sins during their lifetime. Facing a committee of 42 judges, one for each sin, and the great gods Osiris, Thoth and Anubis, they are set on the path to eternity only if declared credible. Yet even now their journey is not assured, as the heart is passed on to be weighed against the ostrich feather of Ma'at, the goddess of truth and balance. If lighter than the feather, the soul is declared fit for the journey into the afterlife. If guilty, it is thrown down before the demonic goddess Ammit, who lives in the Hall of Ma'at. Terrifying Ammit, with her crocodile head, wildcat torso and hippopotamus hind legs, devours the soul so that it wanders anxiously forever, never able to settle, and denied the chance of ever reaching the Field of Reeds.

This spell illustrates the involvement of even the highest gods and goddesses in an individual's journey, and the diversity of deities within the pantheon. It also shows the deities' multifaceted nature for, like people, they could each display both a light and a dark side. Before these deities came to judge the story of a human's soul, pass it fit for eternal bliss, or devour it and condemn it to oblivion, they had their own rich stories to tell.

3

CREATION OUT OF CHAOS

Ancient Egypt's great creator gods dreamed, spoke and blew a life force into the universe, the earth and all that was on it, shaping everything, both natural and manmade. Thereafter, gods and the humans they moulded embarked on a complex relationship, played out in a myriad of myths.

The myths of the great creator gods are mercurial, so that not even the formation of the universe and within it the earth can be attributed to a single method or god. These fundamental myths changed not only with time but also with the persuasions of rulers, the imaginations of priests, and the ongoing ascendancy of one capital city or nome, each with their patron deities, over another.

There is also no knowing which version of events an individual believed in, nor whether a personal preference was set in stone for a lifetime. Many creation myths may not have stood the test of time, either as oral traditions or as written texts, and we will never know their narrative. Some of the given myths may have been cobbled together from different versions of core themes.

OPPOSITE: A bas-relief carving shows creator sun god Re, with a sun disc on top of a falcon head, which linked him with Horus.

Despite this lack of clarity, there is a rich body of creation myths, with strongly portrayed gods at their heart. Most of these were narrated and portrayed in partial form in Pyramid Texts on tomb walls during the Old Kingdom (2686–2160 BCE) and subsequently described in further fragments from the New Kingdom (1550–1069 BCE). It is the fragmentary nature of the evidence that suggests a patching together of some of Ancient Egypt's mythical beginnings.

Creating earth from chaos: the Hermopolitan story

Four great gods with heads in the form of frogs and four great goddesses in the shape of snakes formed the Ogdoad, the eight creator deities of Khemenu, or Khmun. Khemenu was a city-state on the west bank of the Nile in Middle Egypt. It was later named Hermopolis by the Greeks, which meant 'city of Hermes', a deity who was associated with Thoth as well as the Ogdoad.

Thoth, an outsider in terms of the Ogdoad, was nevertheless called Lord of Hermopolis. As a very ancient deity probably

BELOW: **The sun rises from the central mound of creation. Goddesses of the north and south pour away the surrounding waters.**

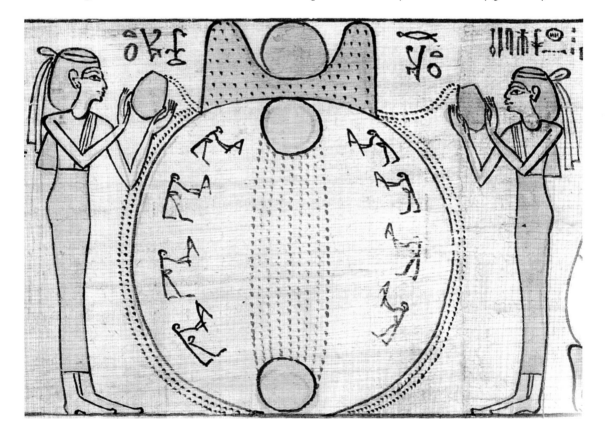

dating back to at least 6000 BCE, Thoth was depicted as a man with the head of an ibis. In one creation myth, a great ibis laid the egg from which the radiant sun god Re emerged to create the world and everything it needed. If Thoth is linked directly with this myth, it explains why, when priests promoted his qualities and elevated his position in the pantheon, he is attached to the other creator gods of the Ogdoad as their 'souls'.

The Ogdoad itself worked in male and female pairs to enable the creation of the universe, the earth, and all that sustains it. Both the frog and the snake were associated with the Nile waters and the miracle of inundation; the frog metamorphosing like magic from a tadpole and the snake emerging as the floodwaters receded, revealing the miracle of fertile soil. In cosmic terms, it might be interpreted that the frog, having transformed from a small wriggling form that swam in the dark, deep, chaotic waters embodied in the god, Nun, could now leap to earth, perceived at the dawn of creation as a mound of soil.

This magical heap of silt, the first patch of dry land in the middle of an unappealing soup, was formed in a number of ways by a variety of gods, but is often attributed to the collective willpower and imagination of the Ogdoad. In Hermopolis, this land was called the Island of Flames.

ABOVE: Ibis-headed creator god, Thoth, is also god of the moon and all knowledge. A shepherd's crook links him with kingship.

THE OGDOAD OF KHEMENU

Khemenu, meaning 'city of eight', was home to the Ogdoad, a collective name for 'eight' given by the Greeks (332–30 BCE). These are some of their qualities and roles.

Amun and Amunet God and goddess of air, breath and energy, later rising to become supreme among the deities of Thebes. Amunet eventually lost her place to the goddess Mut, but Amun, with the sun god Re, became the prime god of Ancient Egypt. In some versions, when Amun and Amunet rose above the other Ogdoad deities, they were replaced by **Nia** and **Niat**, representing emptiness.

Nun and Naunet God and goddess of the fathomless, murky and chaotic waters that covered the universe.

Heh and Hauhet God and goddess of unformed infinity, sometimes seen as invisible currents that rippled through the dark waters of Nun and Naunet, causing chaos. Hauhet also represents positive longevity.

ABOVE: On a wood fragment, the god Heh kneels on the symbol for gold, meaning eternal life.

Kek and Kauket, or Gereh and Gerahet God and goddess of infinite, unnerving darkness and all that is obscured and hidden. Kek is also called the 'bringer of daylight', as his darkness lies closer to dawn, and Kauket the 'bringer of night', being at the edge of sunset.

Eight gods, many myths

Many creation myths, or versions of a main theme, surround the gods and goddesses of the Ogdoad. A common narrative sees the Ogdoad deities in a hands-off creation of the world, pushing out a force through which the Island of Flames at Hermopolis rose from the dark, powerful soup of Nun.

Upon this island a force emerged from a great cosmic egg, also fabricated by the Ogdoad. Unseen at first because there was no light, and therefore also unnamed, it flew out of the egg and became the 'Bird of Light', a characteristic of the sun god, Re. It was he who created everything else – and crucially, he died every day and rose again the next morning. His resurrection and that of human beings, especially rulers, priests and high officials, became a national preoccupation until the end of the kingdom.

Amun and the goose god

The great creator god Amun was also seen as the one who fertilized the egg, using only his breath. Or, unusually, he mouthed a celestial goose that laid the egg from which Re hatched and went forth to fashion the world. This goose, known as Gengen Wer, the 'Great Honker', was revered as a respecter and protector of nature and life. As such, Gengen Wer was blessed with a loyal following of 'ordinary' Egyptians, although his gentle powers swiftly waned. One tradition tells that his shell is buried at Hermopolis. He is depicted with eggs on stelae at Set Ma'at, the 'Place of Truth', now called Deyr al-Medinah on the west bank of the Nile at Thebes.

Over time, as priests elevated Amun and his consort Amunet to the position of prime forces that were independent of the Ogdoad, Amun's creation myths grew in popularity. So too did those of Thoth, who was often seen by his side as an efficient and diligent enabler but was not forgotten as a creator god.

In myth, Thoth, Lord of Hermopolis (later also of the city of Thebes in Upper Egypt), was a stalwart at the right hand of the greatest gods since the beginning of time and, later, the brains and chief administrator supporting Ancient Egypt's kings. Priests elaborated on this narrative, exalting him as a creative, efficient servant and Lord of Scribes, possibly trying to identify with his indispensability in the sight of their rulers.

Thoth was certainly a great god in his own right, but is also closely associated with others from different parts of the kingdom. At times, he was known as the 'Tongue of Ptah', the creator god of Memphis who spoke the world into being. Later, an image of Thoth appears on a doorway to a temple for Amun at Hermopolis during the reign of Seti II (c. 1200–1194 BCE). Thoth appears beside Amun as a loyal companion and servant, wearing his moon god lunar disc and crescent to shine a light over an even greater god.

Formed from a lotus flower

If there is one symbol of Egypt that encapsulates the unfolding of a breathtaking civilization, it is the blue lotus flower, which is depicted in many forms from the

BELOW: Tutankhamun, with 'Amun' in his name, stands by Amun's side in this statue from the king's reign (1333–1332 BCE).

ABOVE: **Rameses II (1279–1213 BCE) offers sacred lotus flowers to enthroned Queen Nefertiti.**

earliest times to the end of the kingdom. Hermopolitan myths tell us that the rising sun in the form of Re, or Khepri the scarab beetle, burst through the opening petals of the lotus at dawn. In one myth, Re went on to create earth. In another, the scarab beetle emerged as a sun child, hushing the newly formed world with a finger pressed to his lips.

A late tradition from the Ptolemaic Period (332–30 BCE) sees the male gods of the Ogdoad setting seed in the perilous sea of Nun. The seed then floated to an egg-shaped ovary, a benen, in the Lake of Fire, where it was fertilized. A lotus flower grew through the egg and, as the petals opened, a boy child emerged. The blue lotus, which rises to the surface of the water in the morning

LEFT: **Lotus flowers and a snake totem are depicted on this ostracon.**

and sinks below it at night, is yet another symbol of renewal and resurrection.

Ptah, the lone creator from Memphis

Ptah was the sole totemic god of Memphis, a city on the Nile Delta near modern-day Cairo, and the only capital of Egypt by the beginning of the second dynasty (2890 BCE). In spite of Ptah's ancient pedigree as god of craftspeople stretching back long before the unification of Egypt, evidence of his myth as a creator is late, from about 700 BCE. Ptah's new role was narrated in the Memphis creation myth on a slab of granite known as the Shabaka Stone, the more archaic language telling the story to the New Kingdom. This is not to say that the myth itself is not older.

Ptah, like some other great gods, created himself. In Papyrus text number 3048, now in the Museum of Berlin, it is said of Ptah that he was: 'A body that created its own body, when heaven did not even exist, and when earth did not exist'.

Having fashioned himself, Ptah moulded the universe, the world and all its features through the thoughts that spilled from his heart and into his mouth, sometimes coughing out gods in his spit. With his hands he crafted living beings, towns and shrines from wood, metal and stone. Depicted as a man wrapped in cloth and a close-fitting cap, rather like a mummy, Ptah's contrasting bare hands highlighted his innate ability to create, and perhaps explains his title as god of all craftspeople.

RIGHT: **A statue (1390–1353 BCE) shows Ptah holding a staff representing enduring power.**

PTAH AND THE POLITICS OF ANCIENT EGYPT

Ptah's powers were so great that in some traditions it was he who imagined and spoke the creation of the nine great gods of the Ennead: the totemic pantheon of Heliopolis. First, Ptah created a wife, Naunet, and together they brought forth Atum, the creator of all other gods in the Ennead. This narrative, which was promoted by the rulers and priests of Memphis, was possibly a way of elevating the reputation of the capital over its neighbour, Heliopolis.

THE ENNEAD OF HELIOPOLIS

Atum Great creator god. As the dynasties progressed, Atum also became associated with and sometimes known as Re, the god of the first light.

Shu Son of Atum and god of light, dry air, and the void.

Tefnut Daughter of Atum, goddess of moist heavy air, and Egypt's protector from the burning sun; like Thoth, she became the tongue of creator god, Ptah.

Geb Son of Shu and Tefnut and god of dry land, which gave the sun god Re a place to rest at the end of the day.

Nut Daughter of Shu and Tefnut.

Osiris Son of Geb and Nut, and the husband of Isis, he was the god of vegetation and, through his epic myth of death and revival, also the god of the underworld.

Isis Daughter of Geb and Nut, and the wife of Osiris. Against all odds, she rescues Osiris from death. Together with Osiris she produces a son, Horus, a nominal tenth member of the Ennead and the empowerment behind the unification of Egypt.

Set Son of Geb and Nut and the husband of Nephthys. Set murdered his brother Osiris and became a disruptor – a god of chaos and malevolence.

Nephthys Daughter of Geb and Nut, Nephthys helped Isis to put Osiris's broken body together before his resurrection.

LEFT: **A gilded wood, faience and glass figure of Geb, god of dry land, was found in Tutankhamun's tomb.**

RIGHT: **Shu wears feathers on his head to show he is the god of wind. He is also god of seafarers.**

OPPOSITE: **Goddess Tefnut stands behind Ptah in the mortuary temple of Rameses II.**

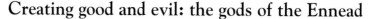

BELOW: **A pyramidion on top of an obelisk represents the mound of creation. Obelisks were erected in pairs, for harmony.**

Creating good and evil: the gods of the Ennead

The cluster of gods named by the Greeks as the Ennead ('The Nine') were the totems of Heliopolis. The Ennead includes deities of judgement in the epic tale of Osiris and Set, the two gods who personified good and evil, peace and war. This is a creation story of a different kind in that it fabricates powerful and often contradictory emotional forces that in turn lead to actions and consequences. The Osiris and Set myth creates an awareness of a conscience that drives the choice between opposite pathways, and the heroism so often found in those who support what is seen to be right.

The Ennead is perhaps a group of gods that creates the psychology of emotional extremes, and a way out of the chaos that these engender. It moulds the idea of a legal system that can maintain harmony in society. Although this seems like a tale of rigid stereotyping of 'good' and 'bad' people, the character of Set becomes more nuanced over time, and very occasionally he assumes the role of protector.

There is no escaping the fact that Set murdered his brother Osiris, and that a way was needed to resurrect him to perpetuate the idea of an eternal god. While the Osiris myth did not create the concept of an eternal life (this was more the province of the sun god, who rose again every day at dawn), the concept of life, death and resurrection in a more human form of god such as Osiris was more tangible to humans and indispensable to kings and their need to seem immortal.

Creating himself: the myths of Atum

Atum created himself through his own force, and one myth tells that having done so he searched for a place to stand in the dark waters of Nun. Atum saw something solid rising above

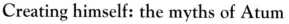

the slimy soup and, stepping on it, realized that it was Mehet-Weret, the cow goddess.

Another myth refers to an island hill that emerged as the Nile waters receded after the annual inundation, and this hill was the land on which Heliopolis stood. Perched on this island, Atum realized the goddess Iusaaset, 'grandmother of all gods'; together they created the god, Shu, and the goddess, Tefnut.

On Pyramid Texts, the creator god, presumed to be Atum, surfaced from the chaotic darkness and slime of Nun as a mythical bennu bird, a phoenix-like heron, who flew to Heliopolis where at dawn he landed on the benben obelisk that represented the rays of the sun. After fashioning a nest of herbs, spices and aromatic woods, he burst into flames but miraculously re-emerged whole and unscathed. As such, he is often seen as the soul of the risen sun god, Re. The capstone on obelisks, the pyramidion, is also called a benben, and is a symbol of rejuvenation and reincarnation, like the sun.

From the Ennead emerges possibly the greatest reincarnation story in Ancient Egypt's mythology: the myth of Osiris.

BELOW: **Horemheb (1319–1292 BCE) kneels before creator god, Atum, whose myth later merged with sun god, Re's.**

The myth of Osiris

Osiris, as the god of vegetation, should have led an important but quiet life perpetuating wheat crops and verdant cattle pasture for the people of Ancient Egypt. Instead, his wisdom and industry led him to become the divine king of Egypt, travelling the world and educating its people about the gods, their roles and the rituals required to respect and honour them. As well as this, Osiris spread civilization across the land, and his benign, generous nature endeared him to all – except his envious brother, Set, who was jealous of the love and respect given to Osiris, and

RIGHT: Osiris is flanked by Isis, his wife, and son, falcon god Horus, on a ninth century BCE gold and lapis lazuli figure.

vengeful towards Osiris's wife, Isis, who was given power to rule Egypt when her husband was away.

Set, determined to rid the universe of his popular brother, constructed a party trick with the help of 72 assistants. Bringing a beautiful, elaborately decorated chest to a banquet, they invited all the guests to lie in it to see whom it would best fit. Unknown to Osiris, Set had made the chest according to his brother's exact measurements. When his turn came, he fitted into it perfectly, at which point Set and his friends snapped the lid shut. The chest, now a coffin, was thrown into the Nile, where Osiris drowned. But the coffin floated out to sea and Isis, devastated but determined, found it stuck in a tree outside the Lebanese port of Byblos. Having returned to Egypt, Isis took care of the body, unaware that Set knew of its return. Enraged, he snatched it and tore it into 13 pieces, which he shared among 13 settlements. But Isis never gave up, and found all but one eye. With the help of her sister, Nephthys, she joined the body together, mummified it, and through the miracle of great gods he was restored. Even while Osiris was dead, Isis performed the remarkable feat of becoming pregnant with their son, the great god Horus.

It would have been a perfect love story, except that Nephthys, sister of Isis and wife of Set, met up with Osiris and in a mist of drunken ecstasy they entwined their bodies together. In symbolism, Osiris, the floodwaters, washed over Nephthys, the red desert, from which sprung a carpet of flowers. Osiris left his lover with a garland of sweet yellow clover, and some say that their union created the jackal-headed Anubis, a god of mummification and protector of the dead. This fleeting passion did not change the nature of Isis, who, ever loving and forgiving, worked with Nephthys in the processes of resurrection.

It is this myth, and other versions, together with the daily renewal of Re, the sun god, that form the basis for the belief in resurrection around which Ancient Egypt's elaborate rituals, priesthood, temples and great pyramids were built. Osiris remained in the underworld as king, while his son, Horus, continued the visceral feud with Set.

Neith, Heka and the Temple of Khnum

The Temple of Khnum, dating to the reign of the Roman Emperor Trajan (r. 98–117 CE), and rising on an earlier one from the time of Tuthmosis III (c. 1479–1425 BCE) was dedicated also to Neith, and to Heka, a god of magic who, as a force of Re, is attributed by some as a creator of the world. The importance of these two deities is manifested by their proximity to Khnum, a great god of inundation, fertile silt and of potters, who scooped out clay from the Nile waters and moulded both gods and humankind on a potter's wheel.

Neith, with so many aspects to her name, was seen as a unifier as well as a creator, sporting the red crown of Lower Egypt and the white crown of Upper Egypt in her regalia. Yet she was also portrayed in some myths as a disruptor through her fashioning of the malicious snake god, Apep. Gods and goddesses were to be both loved and feared.

BELOW: **Most of the Temple of Khnum at Esna, by the Nile in Upper Egypt, was constructed 9m (30ft) below ground.**

Creator of the sun god: Neith

As an ancient goddess possibly associated with North African Berber culture, Neith was seen as both wise and warlike, and as such was symbolized by two arrows crossed on a shield. But as a weaver, she wove the world into being and kept reweaving it every day on her loom. Neith continued as a creator goddess throughout the ages, later associated with the Ogdoad gods. In myth, this association is played out by Neith when she fertilizes an egg with her fluids, producing the sun god, Re, who then adopts the persona of Atum. In his turn, Atum goes on to create more gods from his saliva, and humankind from his tears.

In her role as creator of Re, Neith later became associated with the cow, a symbol of fertility. In one myth she emerges from Nun and metamorphoses from a Nile perch fish, forming a piece of land and standing on it as a newly realized cow. She voices 30 lesser gods, who help her mould the rest of the world once they have transformed themselves into the Ogdoad. Neith is immortalized on the walls of the Temple of Khnum at Esna, about 55km (34 miles) south of Luxor.

The promotion of provincial creator gods

Over time, the unification of Egypt led to a fluid exchange of leading creator gods that broke the strictures of the Ogdoad, Ennead and Memphis pantheons. Led by creative, and at times perhaps crafty, politicized priests and divine kings, gods that were totemic to a particular city or region ranged beyond it and rose in power.

Amun of Hermopolis and Atum of Heliopolis, with Re, god of the sun and Horus or Horakhty, god of the sky, became, with others, major gods in the wider pantheon, spilling outside their creator bases. For some, the boy who emerged from the lotus flower was the god Nefertum, who became the great national god, Atum. For others, he was a young Horus, the product of Re-Horakhty, a glorious melding of two deities that described the god of a rising sun in the infinite sky who were seen as protectors of the entire kingdom.

With the age of creation long gone, the gods of the Ogdoad, the Ennead and the god of Memphis did not disappear without trace. In some traditions, the gods of the Ogdoad lie buried near Thebes at the cult centres of Edfu, Esna and Medinet Habu; in others, they are dissolved into the waters of the Nile, guarding and nurturing the waters forever more. The gods that rose above all others, together with lesser deities in the expansive pantheon, maintained order in the universe, the rotation of life and death in sunrise and sunset, the seasons, and all creatures of the earth, including humankind.

The threat of Nun

The creation of a stable earth from the chaotic slime of the god Nun was never a permanent event. Ancient Egyptians saw as a continual threat the return to Nun, represented by the malevolent snake god Apep, who tried every night to murder the sun god Re, filling the darkness with his hideous roar. In the *Book of the Dead*, the great god Atum warned Osiris that the

BELOW: Karnak Temple Complex is also named, Ipt-Swt, 'Selected Spot', referring to its construction on the mound of creation.

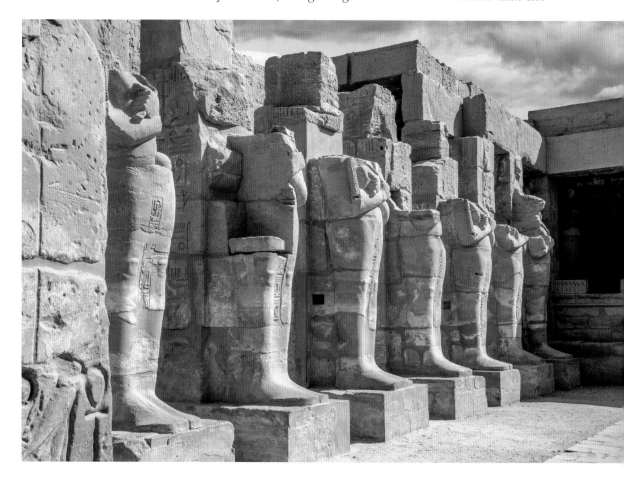

murky waters of Nun would one day rise again, and darkness
would envelop the earth.

On a daily basis, the gods and goddesses of Ancient Egypt kept
the gloom of oblivion at bay for thousands of years. To ensure
their blessings and interventions, priests and people alike praised
and entreated them through rituals, libations, offerings and the
building of great statues and temples. In this way, the sun would
always rise in the morning, the floodwaters would flow every year
and death would never overcome life.

In more prosaic terms, the roles and characteristics of the
gods, so amply played out in myth, came down to earth so that
they could be applied to everyday life. Gods and goddesses in all
their aspects were at work and at play with the people. However,
it took more than the creator gods and goddesses to keep the
wheels of Ancient Egypt turning.

ABOVE: **A bas-relief of
the creator sun god,
Re, shows him sailing
through the dark realms
of the night on a barque.**

4

GODS AND MYTHS IN EARTHLY LIFE

For the average Ancient Egyptian, the creation myths of the great deities were rather removed from everyday narratives. Yet there were aspects of the major gods and goddesses, and countless minor ones too, that addressed the daily practical and spiritual needs of kings and subjects alike, championing their skills and aspirations, and protecting them in their tasks and trials.

Three of the most important values in life were balance, order and truth, which kept chaos and conflict at bay. The goddess Ma'at, who was the arbiter of all cosmological rifts and who kept the heavens stable, was also the deliverer of justice, harmony and peace on earth, in life and in death. Ancient Egyptians were conscious of Ma'at in all they did, whether in their work or personal lives. They took heed of her values so that they could live honorably and with care for all those around them, and for the greater good of their communities, regions and the nation. When they failed, society and the law were not on their side.

OPPOSITE: Harmonious Osiris statues guard the mortuary temple of Queen Hatshepsut, who gave herself the royal name: Ma'atkare.

'Ma'at is great and her work is continuous… She is the path before the inexperienced'. This typical description of Ma'at reinforces two cardinal strengths: her diligence, and her role as a benevolent and dependable guide through life. Ma'at was a stable presence at the dawn of time in the heavens, then on earth, from the grandest palace to the humblest home.

ABOVE: **Ma'at, with a feather of truth in her hair, spreads her protective wings. An ostrich feather sometimes replaces her head.**

In death, Ma'at was key to deciding the fate of the deceased. All citizens would have been familiar with the Osiris myth and his journey through the underworld, around which the ritual processes of judgement in death were created. Here, Ma'at's role was pivotal: she weighed a deceased person's heart against her ostrich feather on a set of scales to test the worthiness of an individual, to see if he or she had led a life of truth and good values.

THE TRUSTED SYMBOLS OF MA'AT

Ma'at, as mother and queen of all gods, is sometimes portrayed with wings attached to her arms but nearly always with a crown, decorated with an ostrich feather that represents truth and order in the world and the cosmos. Her totem is a solid slab of stone, on which she sometimes rests. It represents her dependability: she is a firm foundation that will never crumble, and a symbol of the first island on earth that rose from the chaotic and disturbing waters of Nun. At times she holds a sceptre in one hand and the ankh symbol of life in the other, with weighing scales by her side.

Ma'at, daughter of the sun god Re, is ranked among the highest deities. All gods and goddesses loved her because it was she who kept the wheels turning across the universe through her gracious interventions and judgements. Her mission was one of peace. Bearer of the eight children of the Hermopolitan Ogdoad, she is a mother goddess of some of the greatest Ancient Egyptian gods of all, especially Amun.

Royal respect for Ma'at

On accession to the throne, rulers were required to renew Ma'at, or divine order. This was so that disorder, or *isfet*, caused by the death of the previous king, could be balanced out and harmony restored. This was as important to the citizens as it was to the ruler. In one dramatic renewal ceremony, the sun god Re's barque sails through the sky, with the king playing the role of Re, while Ma'at stands at the vessel's prow. Kings are often depicted holding a statuette of Ma'at in their hands to prove their renewal and allegiance to her. They felt obliged throughout their reign to build and maintain cult temples to demonstrate to her, and the people, their piety.

King Amenhotep III (c. 1386–1353 BCE) declared that it was Ma'at who laid the great creator god Amun on his heart. It was Amenhotep who renamed his vizier Neb-Maat-Re, or Lord of Truth is Re. Even Akhenaten (1353–1336 BCE), who eschewed most gods other than Atem, in an unusual and surprising move during his reign, still pledged his allegiance to Ma'at. She was to be respected, maybe partly because she was as much a goddess of the people as she was of the powerful, which could not be ignored.

But none honoured Ma'at more than Queen Hatshepsut (1473–1458 BCE), who really took to heart another of Ma'at's aspects, as a goddess of peace. Mindful of this, Hatshepsut led her subjects by example in putting this at the centre of her administration. The famous highlight of Hatshepsut's reign is depicted on the walls of the second terrace of

BELOW: Queen Hatshepsut wears a pharaoh's *khat* headdress, and kilt. She is seated, indicating that she receives cult offerings.

her mortuary temple at Deir el-Bahari, part of the Theban necropolis. It shows her peaceful trading expedition to Punt, a kingdom on the Horn of Africa that had not been a commercial partner for more than 300 years.

Hatshepsut's great trek over 1000km (600 miles) brought her face to face with the king and queen of Punt, in a land of gold, ebony and myrrh. Thorny myrrh bushes, which exuded an aromatic resin employed in the embalming of cadavers, in rituals to purify and bless, and as an anti-inflammatory, was associated with Isis, a goddess of healing. For her part, Hatshepsut healed relationships and opened up trade, choosing dialogue and mutual cooperation over aggression.

Queen Hatshepsut was so determined to show her devotion to Ma'at, and therefore to her own commitment to truth and harmony, that she called herself Ma'atkare, which means 'Justice is the soul of Re', the sun god. Her dedication was such that she built the Palace of Ma'at at the great Karnak temple complex at Thebes, with a red quartzite-lined chapel to hold Ma'at's portable barque.

BELOW: In Hatshepsut's Djeser-djeseru, 'holy of holies' mortuary temple, a bas-relief colonnade shows her Punt expedition.

The palace was constructed at the southern end of the temple precinct of Montu. On the face of it, this was an interesting choice of site, since Montu was a fierce falcon-headed sky god of war – the very antithesis of Ma'at. However, looking at the reign

of Hatshepsut, and considering the principles of Ma'at as a healer
of rifts and as one who balances out forces, it makes perfect sense.

Ma'at the giver of earthly power

It was to Ma'at that rulers owed their positions
and therefore their loyalty to her ideals,
though many could not sustain the discipline
required. Following Hatshepsut's death, her
successor, Thutmose III (1458–1425 BCE),
waited about 20 years before throwing the
whole ethos of Ma'at out of the window. In
an unexplained fit of pique, he ordered the
destruction of the queen's images, had her
barque sanctuary smashed, and replaced it with
another in his name. For Thutmose, Ma'at and
her fine balancing of the world through peace
and justice seemed to be an option not an
obligation, even though it was widely held that
contravening her laws would bring chaos and
ruin to the kingdom.

ABOVE: **Thutmose III
built temples to honour
his military expansion
of Egypt, from Syria in
the north to Sudan in
the south.**

How rare Thutmose's actions were among rulers is hard
to judge, and no one knows his motivation. Yet Hatshepsut's
commitment to Ma'at was not wasted, as the legend of the Punt
expedition did not wither, especially among the people. For his
part, Thutmose could not manage to erase Hatshepsut's legacy
totally, as it is said that a gnarled myrrh tree stump that grows
near her mortuary temple on the west bank of the Nile dates
back to her Punt expedition. Her temple is also known as
Djeser-Djeseru, the 'Holy of Holies' – a testament to her loyalty
to Ma'at and her aim to please.

Ma'at and the law of the land

For Ancient Egyptians of all classes, adhering to Ma'at's
principles was a means of providing the glue that bound society
together. As such, it was the basis for codes by which all had to
live and against which everyone was judged in court cases. It is
interesting that a civilization with rigorous legal procedures that
lasted thousands of years had no body of written laws.

There are records of court cases on all manner of disputes and crimes. There are legally binding contracts and bequests. There are documented cases of domestic wranglings, divorce proceedings, assault and murder and seemingly trivial tiffs over donkey hire. Yet nothing suggests that a ream of consistent regulations was applied to any of them.

It is as if every case was perhaps a unique set of circumstances that needed to be verified by witnesses, weighed up and balanced so that a truth could emerge and Ma'at's laws obeyed. Over time, though, a body of precedents built up so that subsequent judgements were not made totally in a vacuum. By the New Kingdom (1550–1069 BCE), statements by the plaintiff, the defendant and witnesses were written on papyri and stored, often in ceramic jars. The cases, evidence and precedents all required recording, and for this there was a very capable god: Thoth. He was a husband of Ma'at, though, like most great gods, he had more than one partner. Together, using Thoth's skills in astronomy and maths, and Ma'at's steady equilibrium, they are credited with charting the path of the sun. For this, Ma'at is often seen as the Eye of Re, enabling the sun god to steer a safe, steady course during the day and night. For Ancient Egyptians, this was an important thing to have done, and possibly gave them confidence in the ability of Ma'at and Thoth to guide viziers, officials and priests towards sound judgements in legal cases, for judges as a separate profession were as yet undefined.

ABOVE: A legal document on parchment lists witnesses called to settle a dispute, essential for achieving the justice of Ma'at.

Protecting the hard-working scribes

Record keeping became Ancient Egypt's greatest tool of justice and administration – two aspects of life necessary for the order that Ma'at required. The written word, democratized somewhat by the Middle Kingdom (2055–1650 BCE) through the proliferation of the papyrus scroll, was churned out by battalions of scribes. Many of these scrolls were the gateway to the masses' access in death through the underworld and into blissful eternity, achieved by negotiating spells that could now be read rather than remembered.

CONTRACTS TO ENSURE ETERNITY

The gods and the afterlife were never far away from consideration, even in the law. In the Middle Kingdom (2055–1650 BCE), an inscribed employment contract between tomb chapel workers and a governor, Djefahapy of Asyut, a city in Middle Egypt, made sure that offerings were made daily and rituals performed to appease the gods in the afterlife. Another contract shows a father's deed of covenant, creating an endowment from which his heirs would be paid to keep his own personal cult permanently maintained. This was a neat way of combining the preservation of his own mortality with provision for his family.

ABOVE: **A contract legalizes a sharecropping arrangement between a landlord and a farmer.**

The scribes themselves were schooled from the age of five and eventually attained high status, as they were numerate as well as literate, and therefore very versatile. Initially, in the Old Kingdom (2686–2160 BCE), scribes were the sons of wealthy officials and others of equal standing, but scribes' skills became so in demand that bright boys, and girls, from poorer backgrounds were enrolled.

Scribes were usually depicted sitting at their writing boards, their reed pens and inkpots in front of them; black ink, the colour of the Nile's life-giving silt, made from soot and gum in one pot and red ink, the colour of life and fire, mixed from red ochre and gum in the other. With these tools, by the Old Kingdom (2686–2160 BCE), scribes shaped hieroglyphs, which developed into quicker, more cursive hieratic script and finally, by about 700 BCE, free-flowing demotic script. Using mainly the black ink, with highlighted or sacred texts in the red, the scribes executed what was considered holy work, documenting *medu netjer*: 'the words of the gods'.

THE SYMBOLS OF THOTH, LORD OF SACRED WORDS

This great creator god was at times symbolized as a man with an ibis head, and at others as the whole bird. A crescent moon, which he is said to have gained by winning a sliver of light from the god Khonsu, sometimes indicates his status as a magical sky god and astronomer. But from the New Kingdom (1550–1069 BCE), it is the writing palette and reed pen that demonstrate his skills, his modernity, and his protection of Ancient Egypt's enormous body of scribes. At times, his ferocious intelligence was symbolized by the head of a baboon.

RIGHT: **In the Papyrus of Hunefer (1300 BCE), Thoth record's royal scribe Hunefer's judgement in death.**

Was Thoth the son of the sun god Re, an ibis who laid the first cosmic egg, or was he created from words? The origins and myths of Thoth, as with most gods and goddesses, changed with time. By the New Kingdom (1550–1069 BCE), his focus had narrowed, and his primary role became Lord of Scribes, or Lord of Sacred Words. So seeing Thoth as a god formed from words was perhaps a neat melding of origin and function, one that was convenient for kings and viziers, and one that all Ancient Egyptians could grasp. When people gave statements in a court of law, they knew that Thoth, the precise wordsmith and record keeper, was the aspect in charge.

Thoth, however, was not alone as protector of scribes. In his aspect as the Lord of Sacred Words, he had a wife other than his creator consort Ma'at, whose skills with reasoning and writing were well matched, if not greater. This goddess, Seshat, meaning simply 'woman scribe', is seen as a quiet, unassuming goddess;

OPPOSITE: **A black basalt statue (c. 2000 BCE) shows a seated scribe with his writing board.**

a sidekick to Thoth. Yet her roles, skills and influence in all classes and situations belie her modest reputation.

Seshat includes in her regalia a headdress with a seven-pointed star in the shape of an upturned bow, though in late dynasties the bow was reinterpreted as a flower. The stars symbolize her cosmic status, and the number seven her accuracy, together with the kind of completion and wholeness that might be applied to a perfect answer to an algebraic equation. The bow shape reinforced her quality of precision and possibly also represented an arc of light, which in this case might refer to knowledge. Seshat's regalia perhaps gave the hard-working scribes some confidence in her ability to protect them on earth. In the heavens, she promised them eternity as a reward for their tireless efforts and service.

ABOVE: **The blue-green of Seshat's hair represents 'protection'.**

On earth, *Per Ankh*, or Houses of Life, were temple libraries that housed a variety of written works, including biographies that ensured their subjects would be immortalized. In these same libraries, scholar scribes met to discuss the countless mathematical and scientific treatises held there.

THE HOUSE OF SESHAT

Seshat had no fixed abode. Cult temples were seen as the real homes of gods and goddesses, and none were built in her name, which also meant that she could not be sustained by offerings of food. Seshat's home and food were perhaps her bank of knowledge, skills and words, which, when written, actually came to life. For her scholarship, Seshat was given, not a home but, as Protector of Librarians, all the libraries and scriptoriums in the world. A copy of every piece of earthly text was lodged in her Library in the Skies.

OPPOSITE: **The chapel walls of painter, Maia (c. 1300 BCE), at Deyr al-Medinah, show the democratization of funerary spells and art.**

Seshat protected them all, and the rich culture and knowledge bank of Ancient Egypt that they represented.

Scribes of the people

It is easy to see how most citizens of Ancient Egypt came to view scribes as gifts of the gods, for their writing and numeracy skills gave them not only access to rituals and spells that helped them through the afterlife, but also to accounting, legal documents and letters both formal and informal. By the First Intermediate Period (2160–2055 BCE), when substantial power was delegated to the nomarchs, the nomes, no longer in hock to the royal capital and its punitive taxation system, grew richer. Wealth trickled down to the ordinary Ancient Egyptian, which meant not only the growth of consumerism and the production of mass-market goods but also purchasing power to hire the skills of the scribes, who could help oil the wheels of their lives, and their deaths.

In handling and seeing text, Ancient Egyptians became more literate, and were therefore able to have more control over their everyday transactions and conflicts with employers, customers, neighbours and partners. The numbers of scribes swelled, but the power of the gods who put them there was in no way diluted. This democratization of literacy, and the documented involvement of gods in everyday life, was made apparent when archaeologists made a surprising discovery at a workers' village, first systematically excavated by Ernesto Schiaparelli in 1905–9.

Ernesto Schiaparelli

Ernesto Schiaparelli (1856–1928) began work as an Egyptologist in 1884. After leading the Egyptian Department of Archaeology at the Museum of Florence, he became Head of the Museum of Egyptology at Turin in 1894, where he amassed an enormous body of finds. Realizing that accruing artefacts was superficial, and that contextual archaeology would create a historical perspective, he concentrated more effort on the actual sites. As leader of the Italian Archaeological Mission in 1901, Schiaparelli excavated the royal tomb of Nefertari in the Valley of the Queens and in 1905 revealed more finds at the nearby workers' settlement at Deyr al-Medinah. However, in 1906, Schiaparelli's newly declared advocacy of contextual archaeology did not prevent him from removing the tomb of royal architect Kha and his wife Meryt, who lived around 1400 BCE, and all their otherworldly goods, to Turin.

The variety of the scribes' functions was revealed through finds discovered in this workers' village, which was set up to construct, paint and adorn the Tombs of the Nobles to the south, on the West Bank of the Nile at Thebes. Deyr al-Medinah was established during the Ramessid period (c. 1295–1069 BCE) of the New Kingdom, and so the thousands of texts written on papyri, and small pieces of flat limestone ostraca, were penned in the more fluid everyday hieratic script.

These texts were not only devotional or legal. Some were sick notes and prescriptions from the local doctor. Another was

RIGHT: Deyr al-Medinah was named Set-Ma'at, or Place of Truth by officials, as its workers were seen as inspired by gods.

a poignant request from a father, asking the doctor for a cure for his son's blindness. One, showing the integral part that the belief system played in the community, was from a scorpion charmer to a priest, asking him for the ingredients for a particular medicine.

Many were letters, seemingly ordinary, domestic letters and requests, which revealed that people from many backgrounds and income groups, both men and women, could read. There are thousands of samples still to be translated and put into context in a village where the huge variety of skills required in royal tomb building would have been represented in a very diverse community.

ABOVE: **An ostracon lists a delivery of groceries to Deyr al-Medinah village.**

Records kept in the manner of Seshat

Seshat's influence on the need for meticulous record keeping matched perfectly the needs of the state, which is exemplified in one of the most informative finds at Deyr al-Medinah. This was a workers' register of attendance over a 280-day period, written, it is assumed, by an official. The register's start date was logged as Year 40 of the reign of Pharaoh Rameses II (1279–1213 BCE). It included the names of each worker, such as Neferabu, Seba, Paser and Pakhuru, and the season of the year for each entry.

Some of the reasons for absence included sad events such as 'Embalming his mother', 'Mourning his son', 'Embalming his brother', and following this, 'Libating for his brother'. These show us how devoted working Egyptians were to the rituals and processes required by the gods. In this vein, another entry merely states, 'Burying the god', which could have been the ritual burying of a statuette to a patron god or goddess. There were also days off for 'Offering to the god' and 'With his god', followed in two incidences by 'His feast'. We do not know if these devotional absences were applauded or censured, but they do seem to have been permitted, thereby reinforcing the idea that the gods were to be respected and appeased, and not just in one's spare time.

Other absences were work-based, explaining why a particular artisan or labourer had been taken away from his usual tasks. This included incidences of incapacity, especially, 'Suffering with his eye', which occurs many times. The 'Suffering of the eye' might seem like a lame excuse, but with the sun's glare, insects and wind-blown dust from the Sahara and from the bricks, stone and ground pigments that construction workers and interior decorators and artists handled, this was probably a common occupational hazard.

LEFT: **This ostracon lists the reasons for workers' absences at Deyr al-Medinah.**

'Fetching stone for the scribe' was a common interruption in the working week, and gives us a picture of the scribe's importance as part of the whole operation. It seems that even the domestic needs of the workers were taken into account, for 'Strengthening the door of his home' and 'Building his house' were logged as legitimate absences. So was 'Brewing beer', the most common drink, and, unlike water, potable, which is of course why it was initially concocted.

Working days taken for mixing cures were seen as a divinely blessed activity, and included 'Making remedies for the scribe's wife' or 'With Khons making medicine'. Khons might refer to the kind and compassionate aspect of the god, Khonsu, son of Amun and Mut and one of the Theban triad, or more likely it was the name of a person, as it was commonly given in honour of the god. Either way, it is an indication of the gods' importance in everyday life.

Wearing kohl for 'Suffering with his eye'

To a certain extent, the cosmetic eyeliner, kohl, protected the eye from the glare of the sun, from dust, and kept insects at bay. Scientific experiments indicate that the lead ions in the kohl induced an immunological response that stimulated antibacterial cells around the eye, giving the eyeliner a medicinal, although ultimately poisonous, property. Worn also to invoke the gods Horus and Re, kohl was seen as a mystical and magical cosmetic that was applied enthusiastically and thickly by workers and wealthy alike. Made from rock minerals, especially galena, which contains lead sulphides, kohl was diluted with a spreading liquid such as oil or gum, and medicinal herbs like fennel and the more precious saffron. The poor added cheap ingredients such as soot and animal fat, while the rich mixed kohl with expensive ground frankincense, gold, pearls and precious gems, each with its own spiritual values.

RIGHT: **This humble clay kohl pot would have held simple firewood ash.**

Away from the workers' register, attention to accuracy and diligence as required by the gods were amply demonstrated by a written legal document at Deyr al-Medinah. It refers to the questionable competence of the vizier in charge of the workforce, whose efforts were not up to standard. Clearly, a job needed to be planned and executed according to the gods' exacting principles, or it would not get done. Ma'at, the goddess of

DEYR AL-MEDINAH AND GODS IN THE HOME

A study by Dr Deborah Sweeney, 'Family Gods at Deir el-Medina' looked in depth at the evidence of three families that lived in the workers' settlement to see whether or not, over several generations covering the Ramessid Period (1295–1069 BCE), they worshipped only one particular 'family' god. Using finds that included text, graffiti, statuettes, stelae and offering tables, the conclusion was that only one family, the Sennedjem, were constant to one god, Amun, and Mut, his wife at this point. Each family covered a broad range of

occupations, from worker to supervisor to scribe, so the samples might signal similar worship patterns among the wider community. It was also suggested that the proximity to Karnak, where Amun's myths and greatness were honoured in feasts, festivals and pageants, might have influenced the Sennedjem family's consistent adherence to the one god.

Ancient Egyptians kept their protective gods with them in all areas of work, as shown on the tomb of administrator, Menna.

harmony, would be disappointed, too. Maybe all was falling apart because calculations for the construction were at fault, in which case there would be turmoil in the heavens, and definitely no principles of Ma'at. Or maybe the calculations and procedures of the task in hand were not recorded to the standards of Seshat.

ABOVE: Seshat, in leopard skin, counts the king's reign on a persea tree. At times she offers kings palm leaves for a long reign.

Recording royal reigns on the Tree of Life

Some say that it was Thoth who counted the years of a king's reign on the leaves of the sacred persea tree. Others say it was Seshat. It is perhaps more logical that this was so, as she completed the job by logging the numbers on a notched palm rib measuring rod, and, as the king's official biographer, recorded all his great deeds. But Seshat was not solely a goddess of the privileged; she also charted the lives of every single citizen.

The sacred persea tree (*Mimusops schimperi*), also called the Ishad, on which a ruler's reign was written, is just one species of a number associated with Ancient Egypt's Tree of Life, a

OPPOSITE: **The Djed Pillar, symbolizing Osiris rising from the dead, and stability, is depicted as a great sacred tree trunk.**

concept that appears in the belief systems and mythologies of other civilizations. In Ancient Egypt, as well as being a royal document, the persea was a symbol associated with creation and continuity, and depicted in numerous forms and media.

The hieroglyph for 'plant', meaning at its heart the Tree of Life, is composed of three sacred blue lotus flowers. The lotus, so deeply rooted in Ancient Egypt's creation myths, is made up of two parts: the bloom and the stems. The bloom, as it opens and

THE SACRED PERSEA TREE

There are many varieties of persea, but this particular one is native to Egypt and Ethiopia. It looks similar to a pear tree in its shape, leaves and blossom, but is evergreen, and therefore, like the goddess Seshat, everlasting and true. Its fruits are oval and green, and the flesh, wrapped around a stone, is juicy and sweet. The tree's sacred status continued through Roman times, as demonstrated by Arcadius, ruler of the Eastern Roman Empire (395–408 CE), who forbade any uprooting, cutting or sale of Egypt's perseas.

RIGHT: **A persea tree is carved in relief on a wall of the Great Hypostyle Hall at the Temple of Amun at Karnak Temple Complex.**

closes daily, represents the myth of the god Osiris as the embodiment of life and the resurrection. The three stems are perceived as the triple trunks of the Tree of Life, always curved to the left. It is said that this is because they were blown by the breath of the creator god, Hu, the Celestial Sphinx with infinite invisible wisdom, who in expelling the sound, 'Hooooch' created the Word of the Gods.

'I am the plant that emerged from Nun,' said the Tree of Life, which grew from the first island of silt that arose from the murky waters of oblivion as the world began, its tips supporting the stars, the moon and the heavens, and its roots delving deep into the dark earth and the underworld. This concept of a large tree rather than the lotus has been identified as the persea in legend, image and engraving, but has also been associated with other tree species, including the tamarisk.

Tamarisk, the saviour tree

After Set had mercilessly employed 72 accomplices to lock his brother Osiris tightly in a coffin, hoping he would drown, the coffin defied Set's scheme by floating out from the Nile and across the Mediterranean. In one version of the myth, it caught on a short, strong bushy tree growing outside the Phoenician port of Byblos. When Osiris's wife, Isis, searched for his coffin, she found it nestling against the tree's sweet-smelling trunk and knew at once that it was the tamarisk.

Isis returned to Egypt with Osiris. Some say that the trunk of the 'saviour' tree became the legendary pillar of Djed, a hieroglyph and central symbol of stability and renewal associated with Osiris and the creator god, Ptah, also the god of carpenters. However, the Djed pillar as depicted in paintings seems too tall and grand to be a tamarisk, and was perhaps another sacred tree, or even a cedar of Lebanon, highly prized as an imported tree used for construction, boat building and furniture making.

The sacred tree of Wepwawet

The tamarisk, also called salt cedar, was an iconic tree to Ancient Egyptians. With white and pink flowers at the tips of feathery branches, it is pretty, but this invasive plant can lose up to 1100 litres (300 gallons) of water per day, so can dry up water sources and deprive other plants of natural irrigation, and is not a plant that animals find good to eat. Yet its power in myth was potent, and it was the tree associated with the forceful god, Wepwawet.

Wepwawet, at first depicted as a weapon-carrying jackal-headed soldier, was unsurprisingly a god of war, although a funerary one.

Yet, as with most gods, his roles were fluid, and the meaning of his name, 'Opener of the Way', signals his job in the underworld as one who opens gates, clears pathways and generally creates a route through the darkness – perhaps chiming with a reference to him in the pyramid texts as one who opened the gap between earth and the heavens.

During the Old Kingdom, Wepwawet was associated with Anubis, another jackal-headed god and an embalmer, who was thought be his son. Later, his cult centre grew around Asyut, known as Lycopolis ('City of Wolves') from the Ptolemaic period (332–30 BCE), though his potency waned and eventually his roles and status, as with so many gods, was taken over by Osiris, god of the dead, of rebirth and of verdant vegetation.

Many trees of the gods

Other trees were in the frame as Trees of Life, such as *Acacia nilotica*, every one of which the spirit of Osiris was said to inhabit, and some say was sacred to Horus, the earthly form of Osiris. The sycamore was seen as the manifestation of the goddesses Nut, Isis and Hathor, who were named the Ladies of Sycamore. This tree, also called Nehet by kings, who grew them around garden pools, was known for its sustaining and popular fig-like fruits. In myth, two sacred sycamores stood at the eastern gate

OPPOSITE: Siase, Royal Scribe and Overseer of the Two Granaries for Rameses II honoured Isis (left) and Wepwawet with this statue.

LEFT: The Papyrus of Henufer shows Henufer's spirit honouring the Bennu Bird, whose home is in the branches of the sacred tree.

OPPOSITE: A sunken wall relief (c. 2250 BCE) at Hathor Temple, Denderah, shows Hapi bearing two vases for the lotus and papyrus of Upper and Lower Egypt.

of heaven facing the sunrise, with Nut and Hathor depicted leaning out of the tree to offer sustenance to the deceased.

Whichever species truly was the Tree of Life, it was the persea that was given the sacred role as the home for the Bennu bird, which sat serenely on its branches. 'Bennu', meaning 'to shine' or 'to arise shining', symbolized the phoenix and the rising sun, symbol of Re. In heavenly terms, Bennu perched in the most special symbolic and sacred tree. In earthly terms, the Bennu sat in its sanctuary in the Temple of Re in Heliopolis.

Eating the fruit of the Tree of Life gave eternity, and crucially, knowledge of the Divine Plan and of the cycles of time that drove the seasons and the great flooding of the Nile. It is here that we pick up Seshat once more, in her roles as astronomer and mathematician. The timing and swell of the annual inundation, the creation of the great steps encased in stone wells that measured the height of the floodwaters, and the monitoring of them as they receded, were all part of Seshat's remit.

The timing of the flood

Seshat worked with Hapi, the god of inundation, to make sure that the annual floodwaters streamed down when the people expected it. At Jabal-al-Silsila in the south of Ancient Egypt, devotees of the god Hapi knelt at shrines, sang hymns and cast offerings into the rising waters. This god of broad girth and swollen breasts was the perfect embodiment of the wealth and fertility brought by the floodwaters, and local Egyptians could identify with Hapi's single garment: a belt around his ample waist that resembled those worn by marsh dwellers. What Hapi actually did, other than appear green to signal new life, we are not sure, but other deities were more proactive in facilitating the all-important inundation.

Satis, the star-gazer

When the goddess Satis looks up at the night sky on the eve of the inundation, she peers at the stars until she sees Sopdet, the goddess of the bright star Sirius, which heralds the flood. Wearing a simple, elegant dress and carrying the ankh of life, Satis waits for the 'Night of the Teardrop', when the great goddess Isis sheds

a single tear for her dying husband, Osiris. Satis reaches out, catches it, and pours it into the Nile. Like the trickle of water that rises in the Ethiopian Highlands, the drop swells into a gushing river. The inundation has begun.

Satis, together with Khnum, the ram-headed and also crocodile-headed Lord of the First Cataract, and Anuket, the Nubian Goddess of the Nile, formed a triad, with each deity bringing their unique qualities to the task of laying down the foundations for a good harvest. Anuket, wearing a crown of reeds and ostrich feathers and with a gazelle running by her side, provided the deep, fertile soil brought down by the floodwaters. With her outstretched arms like the Blue and White Nile that flowed together as one mighty river towards the delta and the sea, she encompassed the great hug that those waters gave Ancient Egyptians when they saw the inundation coming their way.

Over time, this triad, along with many other gods and goddesses, became absorbed by the main deities of the Osiris myth, so that Satis melded into Isis, Khnum into Osiris, and Anuket, Nephthys. The Triad retained an important cult centre at Elephantine Island near the First Cataract, and Khnum, also at the Temple of Esna at Thebes, through to Ptolemaic times (332–30 BCE).

Seshat, goddess of precision

Although Thoth was admired as a god of mathematics, it was Seshat, with her reputation for precision, who shone in accounting and record keeping, especially census taking. By the Second Dynasty of the Old Kingdom (2686–2160 BCE), Seshat is shown taking records of everything from the kings' jubilees, such as the great Sed Festival, to the requirements of military campaigns, their eventual spoils, or cattle inventories.

Seshat is occasionally depicted with a notched palm rib that could be seen as either a timekeeper or a measuring tool. Seshat's proficiency in measurement was crucial for overseeing the most important projects in Ancient Egypt as Goddess of Construction and Protector of Builders. Some schemes, like the construction of cult temples, pyramids and palaces, were carried out for the benefit of gods and godly kings. Others, like the measurement

OPPOSITE: Seshat marks a palm rib on a statue of Rameses II at the Temple of Luxor; in Egyptian, *Ipet resyt*, or 'southern sanctuary'.

ABOVE: **The Rhind Mathematical Papyrus (a 1550 BCE copy), in four rolls, uses tables and formulae to calculate surface areas.**

of the annual inundation of the Nile and the dimensions of irrigation channels, or the delineation of the boundaries of agricultural land, were not only crucial to the ruler's stream of wealth from trading surplus barley and wheat but also the lifeblood of the people.

Seshat and order through measurement

Squeezed between the chaotic desert and the serene Nile, Ancient Egypt relied heavily on the efficient measurement of every cubit of this narrow strip of cultivable soil to feed its ever-growing population. It is no wonder that the accurate surveying and registering of parcels of land was crucial.

All land belonged to the gods; as the king was the embodiment of the god Horus on earth, it was initially under his control, administered through viziers, officials and scribes. Over time, some citizens began to own their land, meaning that they could rent it out to others or even sell it. This was particularly true of mercenary soldiers from outside the kingdom, who had served the country well enough to be rewarded. By the Late Period (664–332 BCE), land ownership by the people was quite common.

Most of the king's subjects, though, farmed the land, grazed it or built on it on a usufructuary basis; this meant they had rights to do with it what they wished as long as they paid taxes in the form of farm produce, which could be hefty. In dividing up this land, Seshat, holding her notched measuring rod, led scribes in applying

BELOW: **A surveyor measures wheat fields for taxation purposes on a tomb wall of Menna, a royal official (c. 1420–1352 BCE).**

their proficient working knowledge of mathematics. From the Rhind Mathematical Papyrus of about 1650 BCE, copied by the scribe Ahmes, we know that this included working out areas, volumes, fractions and even a rudimentary concept of pi.

These skills were totally practical, for it was not until the coming of the Greeks that theories were propounded and the discipline of mathematics was founded and developed. For their part, Ancient Egyptian surveyors always had a huge and never-ending job on their hands, using what now seem to be quite simple albeit effective tools: rods, poles and balls of rope that were unravelled, stretched and knotted to show points where one plot ended and another began.

It seems that kings divided land very equitably. If a tenant lost portions of it to floodwaters, he was able to petition the pharaoh, who sent an administrator to check the loss against the registered plot dimensions, demonstrating how crucial was the accuracy of the initial measurement. In this way, the tenant could receive compensation and extra land. In this instance, farmers would have praised the gods, who protected them in many ways. It is here that we hand over from Seshat, who so ably laid the precise foundations for the systematic production of food, to the great god Osiris, who was the harbinger of the agricultural year.

Osiris, god of agriculture

The Djed Pillar of Osiris, as we have seen, was a symbol of life and resurrection that emerged from Osiris's remarkable story of death at the hands of his brother, Set, and rebirth due to the love and persistence of his wife, Isis. The pillar, stripped of its branches, was also a symbol of the miraculous renewal of lifeless, dry land on the eve of the annual inundation. This was marked by the ceremony of 'Raising the Djed Pillar', which took place on the last day of the month of Khoiak, an auspicious day that marked the end of the old year.

'Djed' comes from the place name 'Djedu', which was situated in Lower Egypt on the Nile Delta. It was from here that the ceremony took place, heralding the New Year and *peret*, the 'Going Forth' or 'Season of Emergence'. During this four-month season, the floodwaters receded and crops could be sown in the

Hathor, sky goddess of motherhood, women, love and patroness of mines wears cow horns and a solar disc.

abundant silt. The Djed Pillar has also been described as the backbone of Osiris, its notches resembling vertebrae. This analogy is symbolically as apt as the tree trunk in describing the great god's stoic qualities – and those of the farmers whose backbreaking work brought in the sheaves.

Hesat, goddess of food and sustenance

Osiris presided over the cultivation of green shoots, both for pasture and for the cereals that provided the mainstay for most Ancient Egyptians: bread and beer. He was ably assisted by other deities, including Hesat. Her name derives from a word meaning 'milk'; she who was originally one of many deities of fertility: a role that transformed into one of sustenance.

Hesat, like Hathor, to whom she is linked, is depicted as a cow with a tray of food between her horns, while milk, often not distinguished from beer, gushes from her udders. She was a goddess of plenty: Ancient Egyptians often referred to beer, the most common drink, as the 'milk of Hesat'. Although an earthly goddess, she was seen as the wet nurse for all other gods, and as a life-giver and sustainer; she even gave birth to and suckled the lugubrious jackal-headed Anubis, god of embalming and the dead. It is said that Anubis's father and Hesat's partner was Re, god of the sun. With Re's life force, *ka*, being identified as Mnevis, the bull god, he, Hesat and Anubis formed an unlikely triad whose cult base was Heliopolis. As with many gods and goddesses, Hesat melded into others over time, so that by the Ptolemaic era (332–30 BCE) she had dissolved into the great goddess Isis.

Food after death

It is in death that we find some of the best evidence of the foods consumed by Ancient Egyptians in life. Complying with rituals affirmed by the gods, foods were taken into the afterlife, ready for the deceased to enjoy there. Of course, royalty, priests and officials of high status took with them the finest and best-prepared ingredients, not to mention wines, both red and white. Mummified foods, especially

YUYA AND TUYU: KEYS TO THE FOOD CUPBOARD

Discovered in 1905 by James E. Quibell, one breathtaking tomb, known simply as KV46, gives us a good insight into the kinds of foods and preservatives used for mummification in around 1400 BCE. The tomb belonged to Yuya and Tuyu, the great-grandparents of King Tutankhamun (1333–1323 BCE). Among other finds were 17 bespoke boxes of food that contained the mummified remains of a range of birds, including geese, and meats: antelope, a leg of veal and high-status beef ribs. These were preserved with an identified expensive resin from a tree related to the pistachio and imported from Syria and Lebanon. Importantly, gods inhaled these resins, so the deceased kings and queens were being equated with them, even in death.

LEFT: **A gilded plaster mask with inlaid eyes of blue glass and quartz covered the head of Tuyu.**

RIGHT: **Yuya's mask is made of cartonnage, which is tight layers of pasted papyrus and linen.**

meats, were slowly dried out and then wrapped in bandages covered with resins to preserve them. Jars of oil and other more liquid foods were stored with them in the tomb. Whether painted on tomb walls, engraved or mummified, all were seen as real.

In the tomb of King Tutankhamun himself, archaeologist Howard Carter (1874–1939) discovered evidence for royal feasts in the afterlife. There were more than 100 finely woven baskets with remains of wheat and barley, loaves of bread, sycamore figs, dates, melons and grapes. There was meat, including ducks, geese and small birds such as pigeons, but nothing like sheep and pigs, which were seen as ordinary fare. In any case, over time, pork became associated with the nefarious god, Set, and was not encouraged as a food for the devout.

Tutankhamun, if he had a sweet tooth, was amply provided for with a jar that probably contained honey, and he could wash it down with fine wine from jars labelled with the grape variety, vintage and vintner. There was no evidence of cake, although we know that the wealthy Ancient Egyptian was partial to it.

As for the worker and his family, their daily fare in this life and the next was much simpler and probably did not include cake. But in a good harvest, their diet was undoubtedly healthy, based as it was on wholemeal bread, with vegetables, pulses, fish and some seemingly lesser meats such as sheep, and birds that were hunted.

RIGHT: A dish of fruit is part of a foodstore for the afterlife in a tomb (c. 1900 BCE) at Deir el-Bahari, part of the Theban necropolis.

God of hunting: the sport of kings

Anhur, the son of the sun god Re, was, like other hunter deities, also a god of war. He was in good company, sharing these two skilled but deadly aspects with the great sky god Horus, multi-talented goddess Neith, and fierce wildcat huntress Sekhmet. These four deities all had heroic tales to tell, which led to their hunter status.

BELOW: Anhu
Sekhmet, so
bore a lion's
This is a bas-
Sekhmet, wi
and cobra cr

RIGHT: **Ancient Egyptian hunters stand on papyrus rafts as they hunt wildfowl with throwing sticks in the marshes.**

In one version of the story of Re's runaway daughter, who was seen also as the Eye of Re and in some instances Tefnut, it is said that she changed into a ferocious lioness, the goddess Menhet. With this new aspect, Re's daughter gained the strength, courage and knowledge to run southward across the grasslands and thornbush to Nubia without being attacked by other wild animals. Re, missing his daughter terribly, sent out a party to find her. At the head was a remarkable hunter, who found her and brought her back. Re was so impressed that he gave the hunter the name Anhur, and offered him his daughter's hand in marriage. It is not known how his daughter's fierce goddess

aspect Menhet reacted to this. Anhur, although a suitor to
Re's daughter, was also seen as his son; a common complex family
situation in Ancient Egyptian mythology and reality.

Feasts for kings and protein for the poor

Although many gods and goddesses included birds and animals
in their regalia, Ancient Egyptians had no qualms about
hunting these same creatures, which, after all, were gifts from
the heavens. But like every other aspect of society, hunting was
an occupation divided by class. While the poor were allowed
to supplement the protein in their diet with wild birds such as

ducks, geese, quail and cranes, it was a privilege of royalty and the supreme elite to hunt big game such as leopards and lions, wild cattle, ibex, gazelles and ostriches.

In predynastic times, hunters found plenty of prey in the Nile Valley, but during the Old Kingdom (2686–2160 BCE), the rich fauna of the delta became unavailable when marshlands were drained for agriculture and settlement. This meant that hunters wanting more than small birds had to look to the harsh desert.

For the worker, who was time-poor, the remaining wetlands were usually enough for him to bag some waterfowl using spears, bows and arrows, throwing sticks and nets. Kings, however, indulged in group hunting, led by a head hunter and using

ANHUR, WITH THE REGALIA OF A KING

Anhur can be seen dressed as a king, striding along in his feather-patterned skirt; his head crowned with a snake and four long feathers. At times he is shown with a hunting or a fighting lance in one hand and a rope in the other – perhaps for catching Re's daughter, although it is as likely to represent the snaring of prey or enemy captives. A brave god, he was one of the deities who stood at the prow of the celestial barque defending Re against the snake god Apep as he travelled through the night of darkness and death. For this and other ways in which Anhur shook off Re's enemies, he was given the name 'Slayer of Foes'. Anhur might have been greatly feared, but at his annual festival a light-hearted mock battle took place between local priests and the people. During the Late Period (664–332 BCE), Anhur was melded with Shu, the creator god of air, who was also attributed with rescuing Re's daughter.

LEFT: **This Late Period statue shows king-like Anhur, holding a staff and with a crown of four feathers on top of a wig with a uraeus.**

beaters. By the New Kingdom (1550–1069 BCE), chariots were
a well-established means of royal and military transport, and
took the royal party on hunting trips, which often led them to
waterholes in the evening, where animals gathered, exposed
to the volley of arrows released on them. It was here that great
game were triumphantly killed, and their skins used as trophies,
clothing and soft furnishings of the wealthy.

Evidence from tomb paintings shows us that Ancient
Egyptians were also familiar with creatures that were not native
to their territory, indicating that kings and high officials kept wild
animals, probably for hunting; there is some evidence that they
tried to breed them. Queen Hatshepsut kept baboons, giraffes,
cheetahs and exotic birds imported from Punt on the Horn of
Africa, though we do not know whether these were for hunting
or as pets – Ancient Egyptians did keep animals, especially dogs
and cats, in the home.

God of hearth and home

While Khnum was the great god of procreation and fertility,
having spun humankind from clay on his potter's wheel, a more
down-to-earth god was at work in the home, championing people
and pets alike. Bes was a small demonic god of war with a heart of
gold, for he was fiercely protective of women, children and, with
the hippopotamus goddess Taweret, attended women in labour, as
evinced by artworks in birthing houses.

Bes was also a warm protector god of the fabric of the house,
and so loved that he was depicted on many everyday items, from
cosmetic palettes and ointment jars to furniture and especially
knives. Countless amulets were made in his image, which was
as a comical, sometimes lion-like, bearded dancing man with
prominent genitals to indicate fertility, sticking his tongue out
and shaking a rattle. It is the rattle and his humorous pose that
give clues to Bes's role as god of safe birth, protector of babies
and, it seems, child entertainer. It is said that he guarded the
young Horus, who was born of Isis and the deceased god Osiris;
because of this, Bes was deemed more than capable of taking care
of young human beings and their mothers.

ABOVE: Figurines of Bes were often placed by the door for protection, and his image was sometimes even tattooed on the skin.

OPPOSITE: A nineteenth dynasty statue of Ptah, god of craftsmen such as carpenters and sculptors, stands in the Karnak Temple Complex.

Bes was a god of old but came to the fore from the New Kingdom (1550–1069 BCE) and grew in popularity through to Roman times (30 BCE–395 CE). Although this is contentious among some Egyptologists, it has been suggested that he originated from another African pantheon, and certainly the mischief-maker/protector spirit has featured prominently in many other African cultures.

Bes is linked with other gods, such as Hathor, also a guardian of hearth and home. By Ptolemaic times (332–30 BCE), Bes had more or less melded into his wife, or maybe his female aspect, which in any case looked rather like him. Whether as Bes or Bestet, he and she were fiercely protective of the homes of all Ancient Egyptians, on whose walls their images were often depicted.

Homes for Bes

Bes resided in even the humblest home, which changed from papyrus reed construction in and around the Nile Delta in predynastic times to sun-dried clay bricks mixed with straw and dung – materials that were more permanent and appropriate to a growing, more urbanized population. The poorest families constructed homes with single-skin walls, while wealthier workers were able to build them with double and triple skins, increasing insulation against both the heat and the cold. Stone was a material for the wealthy alone, although their simple post and lintel structures continued long after the revolutionary arch came into play from the fourth dynasty in about 2613 BCE. The highest officials of the land could boast grand mansions, some with as many as 70 rooms, with orchards, pools and gardens. Whether large or small, grand or humble, images and statuettes of gods and goddesses were part of the décor and seen as necessary protection.

Homes expanded to two or three storeys, with flat roofs as extra living space. Those that were not clustered closely together in cities were set in compounds with courtyards and gardens surrounded by chambers. With at least three rooms, Ancient Egyptians had some space to fill with furniture that made life more comfortable, and for the wealthy, more opulent. For this, Ancient

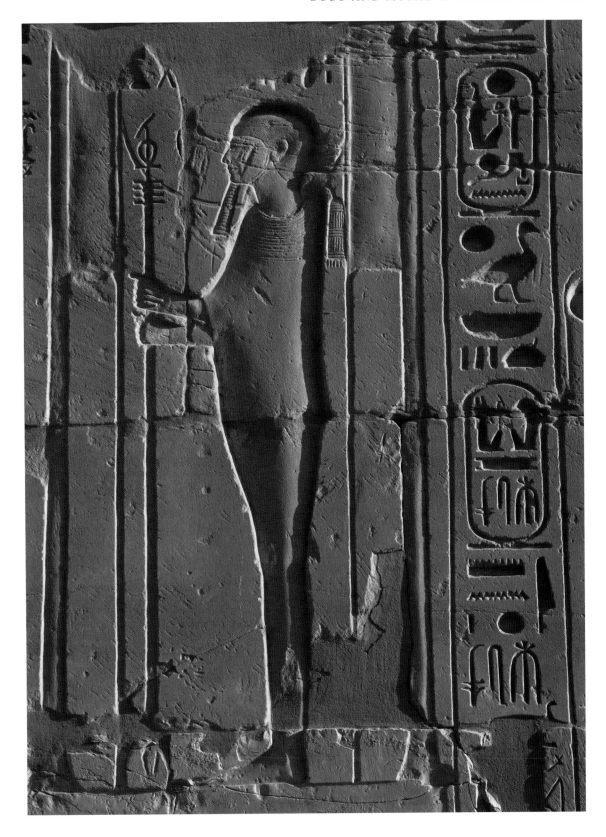

ABOVE: **The chair of scribe Reniseneb (c. 1450 BCE) is veneered with ivory. An ivory decoration shows him royally sitting on an identical one.**

Egyptians relied on Ptah, the great god of carpenters, after whom Egypt itself was named. Carpenters, who often worked together in community or royal workshops, toiled in the knowledge that Ptah could be called upon for protection and help.

From the Middle Kingdom (2055–1650 BCE), furniture for the wealthy began to look like pieces we might use today. Fine wooden beds with legs, headboard and a stuffed mattress, chests, tables and four-legged stools topped with leather and skins became the norm, and not only in the palaces of kings and the homes of viziers. Senior scribes and officials could enjoy the comfort of them, too. Expensive imported woods, such as cedar from Lebanon and ebony from Nubia and the Horn of Africa, with veneers, ivory inlays and other intricate work, made each piece a desirable object in its own right. As for the workers, they too had furniture: low wooden stools with reed seats or floor matting to sit on and eat at, reed chests and baskets for storage, and straw or wool-filled mattresses for beds.

SLEEP BLESSED BY THE GODS

Ancient Egyptians relied on gods such as Bes and Taweret to protect them through the dark and dangerous night. For this reason, their names were often inscribed or engraved on headrests. These timeless wood or stone 'pillows' lifted the head so that the gods would make sure that the sleeping person would rise again the next morning. On a practical note, they allowed air to circulate on a hot night. In death, miniature headrests were often bound together with the mummy to ensure that the head would stay uplifted for the moment of resurrection, and that it would not fall off while the deceased made the journey through the underworld.

RIGHT: **Hands hold up either side of this headrest, dated about 2125–1975 BCE. They are used in other parts of Africa.**

Keeping clean was very important to Ancient Egyptians, in both life and death, and it seems that they did not need a god or goddess to help them with the task. However, early water sources – the Nile, oases and canals – were not always the purest. From the New Kingdom (1550–1069 BCE), though, the wealthy were able to draw from wells within their own compounds, which many could use in their indoor bathrooms, the most affluent with copper plumbing, while the poor sometimes had access to community wells. Both, though, shared waste water disposal methods, which at best were cesspits dug for the purpose and, at worst, the river or the streets.

While sanitation was not at that point on the radar of most Ancient Egyptians, a preoccupation for all families, whether rich or poor, was the health and wellbeing of its members. In Ancient Egypt, this was the province not only of physicians but also of priests and priestesses, for the physical and the spiritual were inseparable. To help them, they needed holistic input from apothecaries and magicians – and of course, the powers of deities such as the fierce but healing goddess, Sekhmet.

ABOVE: Cleopatra VII is said to have used this bath at Kom Ombo Temple. A wood fire heated the water from a tunnel beneath.

5

PRIESTS, PRIESTESSES AND FESTIVALS FOR THE GODS

The myths of Ancient Egypt weave an intricate web of cosmic power that changed from predynastic times through to the Roman period. Over these millennia, priests and priestesses, the cults of gods and goddesses and the power of kings were woven together in a symbiotic pattern, rising and falling with the fortunes of the state of Ancient Egypt.

Priests and priestesses began their complex and often mystical craft in a small way. Long before they served the high gods and goddesses of the great kingdom of Ancient Egypt, they administered the needs of local cult deities, who grew into revered totems of regional nomes. Based around successful city-states, these provinces were ruled by nomarchs who sported the

OPPOSITE: Hathor leads Horus at Dendera's Temple of Hathor. In the Nineteenth dynasty, its High Priest Nebwenenef was famed for his power.

regalia of the totem, giving them a spiritual power in the eyes of the people, and their neighbouring rivals. The priesthood began to serve the ruler as much as the deity.

When kings became gods and high priests

All changed, albeit incrementally, around 3150 BCE, when power was centralized, and with it the priesthood. Horus the falcon god, who might have been either the older brother or the son of the great god Osiris and the goddess Isis, entered the realm of humankind to forge a bond between Upper and Lower Egypt. In this way, the kingdom of Egypt was created and the unifying power of Horus was embodied by a human ruler or rulers, who could have been Narmer, Menes, Scorpion or perhaps a melding of all three.

In history, this earthly king was attributed with the unification of Egypt. From then on, he and all subsequent kings and queens bore the insignia and serekh hieroglyph of Horus. Ruler and god became one in the same being. The king or queen was an earthly representative of all gods and goddesses, served by high

BELOW: **A Nineteenth dynasty bas-relief of High Priest Amenhotep-Huy, Director of the Osiris Festival, shows him receiving offerings.**

TEMPLES TO HORUS

Over the whole span of Ancient Egypt's long history, many cult temples were devoted to Horus. Here, priests led the winter solstice celebration identified with him. He had many gifts, roles and auspicious physical traits. Although sometimes eyeless, his right eye when in place was seen as the sun or the morning star, and his left eye as the moon, which made him especially powerful in the heavens.

Horus had practical value, too, as one of several deities who could alleviate insect stings and snake bites. Priests conducted rituals, ceremonies and festivals appropriate to each aspect, especially at main cult sites that included Letopolis. This ancient city celebrated Horus in his eyeless state, when he was a very aggressive god, yet a patron of the blind. At Hierakonpolis, 'the city of the Hawk', Horus was honoured as his regal, uniting self, while Behdet, 'the town of the sun disc', is seen as the site of the great battle between Horus and Set. Behdet is now known as Edfu, and is renowned for its temple to Horus, which was beautifully refurbished in the Ptolemaic era (332–30 BCE).

As high priest or priestess, the king or queen was in charge of every cult shrine and temple and all they contained, from stele and statues to altars and offerings. As rulers could not be in all temples at once, more earthly varieties of priest and priestess administered to the needs of gods and goddesses in temples, which were considered the real homes of the deities.

ABOVE: **The enduring image of Horus guards the sandstone Temple of Horus at Edfu, built in the Ptolemaic Period (332–30 BCE).**

priests and priestesses, some of whom rose to godly status, too. The priesthood served deities either as individuals or in clusters, usually of three great gods. These often comprised a father, mother and son, making a triad of generational continuity, and therefore a very powerful cult force. Great temples were often built around these triads, and the priests who served them became very powerful.

Serving gods, kings and Ma'at

Priests served the needs of gods and goddesses in the names of kings and queens on a daily basis. This was not only to please their ruler and cult deity but also – and probably most importantly – to make sure that the principles of the god Ma'at were maintained. Harmony, balance and order in the heavens and on earth were the primary requirements of this god; without

RIGHT: **Priestly offerings honour Re-Horakhty, a rising sun fusion of gods Re and Horus, on wood, at Deir el-Bahari (c. 900 BCE).**

them, chaos would reign in both realms. There would be turmoil; floods and harvests on earth would fail, the kingdom would collapse and the priests would be out of a job.

Priests smoothed the way between earth and heaven; life and death. They were masters and mistresses of ceremonies, though not of any kind of religious service that we might see examples of today. It is easy to pin our ideas of priesthood on to another belief system, but in Ancient Egypt priests were for a very long time celebrants only of a sacred inner sanctum, not of a community.

To keep order in the universe, a cult priest or priestess treated the deity as a human being, making sure the statue that embodied the god or goddess was woken in the morning, washed, perfumed, clothed, adorned and given breakfast. Ritual chants were performed in his or her honour, and offerings and libations made. It was a very private affair and ordinary citizens were for the most part shut out. Their daily connection with gods and goddesses revolved around rituals in the home, honouring statuettes, or wearing amulets on the body.

Ordinary citizens were sometimes seen in the courtyard outside a main temple building, where they could lay offerings and libations in the hope of answers to their problems, but their entry into the temple buildings was barred. Their closest interaction with the gods came during festivals – and happily for ordinary folk, there were plenty of those. Many kept the myths of the gods alive, restoring relationships between the deities, and between them and the people.

The festival of the 'Good Meeting'

Priests restored the relationship between Horus and one of his consorts, Hathor, on an annual basis.

Re, the great sun god, gazed southward at the Kingdom of Nubia and spied the warlike, bloodthirsty lioness Hathor. In a move to subdue her, and probably her territory, he sent Shu, the god of air, and Thoth, the god of wisdom, to persuade Hathor to travel to Egypt. Once there, she became the gracious, peaceful wife of Horus, and a symbol of love, the home and pleasure. No one knows how easy Horus was to live with – after all, he was a prominent and busy god – but Hathor only managed to

BELOW: **Priests process at the Festival of Min, fertility god, on a relief from Rameses III's mortuary temple.**

visit him once a year. This annual renewal of their relationship was celebrated in the festival of the 'Good Meeting', during which Hathor's statue was processed from her totemic home of Dendera to the Temple of Horus at Edfu.

Specialist priests and part-timers

Over time, most large temple complexes were controlled by a very powerful high priest or priestess: the *hem-netjer tepi*, or 'primary servant of the god'. Working a tier below them were specialist astronomers, who as 'hour' priests could predict auspicious days, and *sem* priests who served rituals for the deceased, embalming them and chanting spells. This core priesthood, together with musicians and a choir, were assisted by teams of part-time priests and helpers, who rotated their service on a monthly basis.

Taken from well-paid craftsmen's families or high-status, educated elites who held down good civilian jobs, these part-timers adopted several important roles. '*Wab*' priests, usually from the skilled working class, maintained the temple and the sacred barque. They prepared festivals with temple chefs and other 'outsiders'. Educated 'lector' priests, the *hery-heb*, copied religious and other texts that filled the libraries: the Halls of Life. Although unpaid in the temple, most part-timers had well-remunerated state jobs, and took a share of the sumptuous temple offerings made to the gods.

Whether they were full- or part-timers, we owe a great deal to priests: as scholars and librarians, they gave us some of the keys to our knowledge of Ancient Egypt. In the Ptolemaic era, priests became the historians and early anthropologists of Ancient Egypt, putting together genealogies of kings and aspects of the deities, and enabling us to date the ongoing processes of change for gods, goddesses and their myths.

ABOVE: *Sem priest Imeny's stela for Senruset III (1836– 1818 BCE) shows goddess Hathor offering kingly Horus the sign of life.*

Priests and the art of astrology

Priests were astronomers and also astrologers, able to pinpoint auspicious times of the year for the king. They believed that every Ancient Egyptian's life was governed by their position within the zodiac calendar.

The Egyptian horoscope was divided into 12 signs. One sign was named for the River Nile; the other 11 were named for gods and goddesses: Amun-Re, Mut, Geb, Osiris, Isis, Thoth, Horus, Anubis, Set, Bastet and Sekhmet. While the months that each sign represented were slightly different from ours, the idea of the 12-sign zodiac is similar to that used by today's astrologers.

Priests also worked out the planets' characteristics. Therefore, (though this could vary), Venus was the morning deity; Mercury, the stationary, or inert; Mars was Horus, the red one; Saturn, Horus the bull; and Jupiter, Horus who uncovers the mystery.

BELOW: Egyptian and Greek astronomies meet on a 50 BCE zodiac at Dendera. Taurus equated to Osiris; Aries to Amun and so on.

CHIEF FLORIST TO THE TEMPLE

As told in the Great Papyrus Harris, Rameses III (1187–1156 BCE) designed 'a sacred way, splendid with flowers from all countries'. Lise Manniche, in her book *An Ancient Egyptian Herbal* (1989), calculated that he made more than a million floral offerings at the Great Temple of Amun at Karnak alone. This demonstrates the importance of plant life to Ancient Egyptians, and the crucial role of the chief temple florist.

The scent, colour, form and sometimes medicinal properties of flowering, climbing, fruiting and foliage plants were all considerations in making perfumed oils and sacred bouquets, wreaths, garlands and collars as offerings to gods and kings alike. Festival processions were adorned with favourite and auspicious flowers: lotus, lily, iris, rose, cornflower, anemone, daisy, chrysanthemum, and climbers: pipevine, black bryony, smilax and even the mandrake, the properties of which could kill or cure. Twists of papyrus and lotus flowers are a common motif on tomb walls and engravings to symbolize the unification of Ancient Egypt.

ABOVE: A king, also the chief priest, makes an offering of papyrus flowers to the gods. Kings tied flowers even to their war chariots.

Bringing out the gods

Priests and priestesses' roles during festivals were a marked contrast to the daily routine, and involved organizing celebrations that could last for days or even weeks. Each cult deity was honoured annually with its own local festival, while gods and goddesses who drove the success of the nation, through great works such as the annual inundation and the harvest, were celebrated by the whole population. These gave the priesthood hard work but also kudos, as they organized processions of their brightly adorned temple statue, parading it on a sacred route that often included the Nile, accompanied by music, singing, dancing, crowds of ordinary folk, and garlands and posies of perfumed flowers.

There was a difference between the smaller cult temples and the great complexes such as Karnak. The priests here grew in status until, by the New Kingdom (1550–1069 BCE), many were themselves seen as gods. The festivals they conducted, such as the king's Heb Sed jubilee, or Amun and Mut's Opet festival, were grand promotional affairs. On these occasions, enormous, lavishly adorned statues were placed in model barques decorated in gold and bright, meaningful colours. *Wab* priests carried them in great solemnity, walking with an enormous entourage led by the king along a route that took in a spell along the great River Nile, where the model boats were transported by a procession of real ones, including the royal barque.

RIGHT: A bas-relief adorns Eighteenth dynasty Thutmose III Festival Hall, built for his Heb Sed jubilee and, after, the Opet festival.

Packing the route were throngs of citizens, following the procession and enjoying the pageant of colour, music, dancing and flowers, which renewed the peoples' relationships with powers both earthly and heavenly. Along the choreographed pilgrimage route, the processions stopped at auspicious way stations where the deity would rest, libations and offerings would be made, and oracles would pass judgement from the gods, or offer advice on their behalf.

Oracles and the priesthood

Oracles were an age-old way of receiving messages, hope and help from the gods. They were not confined to those of means, especially after the First Intermediate Period (2160–2055 BCE), when Ancient Egypt's belief system showed signs of decentralization and democratization. From the New Kingdom (1550–1069 BCE), oracles became part of the judicial system, and were consulted to help discover the truth in a dispute. Priests at this time were occasionally involved in court cases as part-time judges, so, together with oracles, the role of gods had a firm place in the execution of justice. From the Third Intermediate Period (1069–664 BCE), the oracle was consulted by local rulers to help with decision-making, especially in Thebes and around the oases and delta areas.

Evidence for festivals

Ancient Egyptians may not have left us with much detailed evidence of festivals, but they did at times list them, although changes were made down the years as gods and goddesses rose or fell in favour. During the Old Kingdom (2686–2160 BCE), a festival calendar beginning with the New Year was often engraved on the doorjambs and lintels of royal and other high-status tomb chapels. They showed that following on from the Opening of the Year, which celebrated the imminent inundation and took place in the twelfth month, came the Festival for Thoth, First of the Year, Wag Festival, Sokar Festival, Great Festival, Flame Festival, Procession of Min and the Sadj Festival. We do not know exactly what some of these entailed, but we get a sense of the festivals revolving around the natural forces that shaped the farming year.

As with festival details, it is in the New Kingdom that other evidence of lists and deities involved emerges. Some are described on ostraca at Deir al-Medinah. There are rock inscriptions at Jabal-el-Silsila, and a great festival calendar at Medinet Habu for Rameses III (1187–1156 BCE). Thebes, once the capital of Ancient Egypt, provides more information through evidence found in its temple decorations and inscriptions than any other city or region, which may give us a lopsided idea of the range of festivals and gods and goddesses celebrated. What is certain is that wherever and whenever they occurred, most festivals were a combination of praise and pleas for times of plenty.

Descriptions of festivals for gods and goddesses in image and writing are often patchy. Again, evidence dates from the New Kingdom (1550–1069 BCE) onwards, and is apparent for the festivals dedicated as much to kings as gods, particularly the Heb Sed festival, which marked a long reign – or sometimes, it seems, rejuvenated a short one. That the king was also seen as a god meant there was a fine distinction between a secular and a religious festival. Gods, though involved in the festival, did

BELOW: **A festival calendar decorates a wall at Rameses II's temple at Abydos. Copies of calendars on scrolls were kept in temples.**

not appear to be the main focus, and their myths seemed to be
subsumed by the creation of the king's own.

Opet, the Beautiful Feast

The New Kingdom (1055–1069 BCE) was a time for new
ceremonies, the most elaborate of which was Opet. Commonly
called the Beautiful Feast, it took place around the second month
of the inundation. At this festival, the great god Amun-Re's
powers were renewed in the king or queen's *ka*, their deep soul,
reinstating their right to divine kingship and at the same time
giving birth to a fresh year. Wall paintings show us the riches
lavished upon the royal and godly procession of Amun-Re and
his barque from Karnak to Luxor. The festival was a marked
contrast to the simple blessings scattered on the Nile for Hapi,
and grew into a joyful celebration for all citizens. In the twelfth
century BCE, it is recorded that on one occasion at Opet, the
hard-working temple officials distributed 11,341 loaves of bread
to the people, and 385 flagons of beer.

Sun, moon, stars, priests and the festival calendar

When the goddess Seshat aligned the moon, stars and sun to
create the calendar, she got it nearly right but not quite; her
calendar year was just short of the 365.25 days required to

ABOVE: Acrobats
perform backbends,
and musicians play, as
they process along the
Third Pylon at Karnak
Temple Complex.

make dates consistent. Consequently, festival days shifted back slightly every year, meaning that even those that marked the inundation and harvest were held in months at odds with their actual occurrence. This did not faze rulers, though it might have put pressure on priests, officials and scribes, who had to make sure that the masses turned out in full to watch them.

As festivals were often the only public fun that working men and women had, they would have been eager to attend in any case. Some ceremonies, though, marked anxious times, such as the June inundation, when Sopdet, the goddess of the star Sirius, arose to herald the beginning of the year, and the start of the festive timetable. That Sopdet missed most of the ceremonies because her star rarely aligned with the inundation did not detract from her mythical presence

At this time, when the rains were reaching the Nile, some very simple rituals took place; libations, offerings and flowers were sprinkled into the flowing waters of the great river to please gods such as Hapi, bringer of the floods. That no one could predict the success or otherwise of the inundation at this point gives us an idea of the precariousness of life and an understanding of the more elaborate farming festival rituals that followed through the seasons.

Festivals of flood, farming and fun

Hathor, goddess of the Milky Way, was celebrated as a life-giving sacred cow, who gushed milk and mothered the nation. Her generosity of spirit and boundless love and happiness made her

A CALENDAR OF CELEBRATIONS

The importance of festivals in Ancient Egyptian life is indicated by the names of the months in the calendar, for the prefix '*pa-n*' means 'the festival month of'. There were up to five epagomenal days, with an occasional sixth; these were days slotted between the months to make up for the slightly shortened calendar. The main five became the birthdays of some of the most celebrated gods and goddesses who lasted through to the Roman period (30 BCE–395 CE):
Day 1, Osiris; Day 2, Horus; Day 3, Set; Day 4, Isis; Day 5, Nephthys.

Egyptian name	Coptic name	Dates
Dhwty	Thout	29 August –27 September
pa-n-ipAt	Paope	28 September–27 October
Hwt-Hr	Hathor	28 October–26 November
kA-Hr-kA	Koiakh	27 November–26 December
tA-aAbt	Tobe	27 December–25 January
pA-nmxr	Mshir	26 January–24 February
pA-n-imn-Htp	Paremhotep	25 February–26 March
pA-n-rnnwtt	Parmoute	27 March–25 April
pA-n-xnsw	Pashons	26 April–25 May
pA-n-int	Paone	26 May–24 June
ipip	Epep	25 June–24 July
mswt-ra	Mesore	25 July–23 August

(From von Beckerath, 1980 (Egyptian months) and Cody, 1991 (Coptic months))

the perfect goddess of festivals. Hathor's sacred colour, blue-green, represented the growing shoots of new life and therefore fertility and farming. As the goddess of dance, music, instruments and passion, her role in festivals was often one of fun.

Yet, as the Lady of the West and of the Southern Sycamore, Hathor was there for everyone at their time of death, offering water to the deceased from the sycamore tree, and milk from its sap, which had once helped to restore Horus's sight when the violent god, Set, tore at his eyes and blinded him. Associated with perfume and myrrh, Hathor's presence was there at the ritual washing and embalming of the body. For these aspects, Hathor was also a goddess for the injured and the dead, and the ceremonies that honoured them.

Hathor's celebratory characteristics and roles reflected the broad range of Ancient Egypt's many festivals, from serious ceremonies for gods, goddesses, kings and the cosmos to fun days celebrating everything from birth to beer. As a framework for festival days, or sometimes weeks, the farming calendar provided auspicious times of the year, and punctuation marks between work and rest. *Akhet*, the season of inundation between June and September; *peret*, the sowing and growing season between October and February; and *shemu*, harvest time between March and May, provided a triad of different rhythms and tangible outcomes upon which so many festivals were based.

RIGHT: **Goddess Hathor is depicted as a sacred cow, with a solar disc and uraeus crown on this Late Period (664–332 BCE) fresco.**

THOTH'S CEREMONY ON THE EVE OF THE INUNDATION

During the inundation in August, an invocation at dawn on the Day of Going Forth of Thoth was made to please this god, who, through his mathematical ability, could time the floodwaters on which Ancient Egyptians depended. The invocation gives the great gods a secrecy that could only enhance their untouchable power.

Such was all-knowing Thoth,
who saw all things,
and seeing understood,
and understanding has the power to disclose
and to give explanation.
For what he knew he engraved on stone;
Yet though he engraved them on to stone
He hid them mostly.
The sacred symbols of the cosmic elements
he hid … keeping sure silence,
that every younger age of cosmic time might seek for them.

(*Kore Kosmou* or '*Virgin or Eye of the Cosmos or the World*', adapted from translation by G.S.R. Meade

RIGHT: **The Papyrus of Ani shows Ani, a scribe, with wife Tutu, adoring Thoth (left); and preparing offerings for him (right).**

Ritual seed sowing at the Khoiak festival

Khoiak is the Coptic name for an ancient festival that took place in the fourth month of the inundation, when the waters had retreated and the soil was damp and fertile. It celebrates the hope of a good outcome for the year's crops and pastures and blesses

the god Sokar, a multitasking deity who, among other things, was responsible for agriculture, an aspect that led to depictions of him with farming tools.

The rituals played out a series of events around the myth of Osiris, whose birth and death mirrored the cycle of crop growing and harvesting. Highly

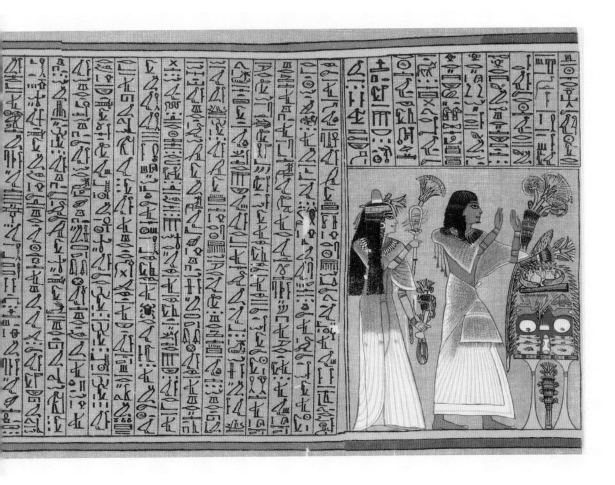

developed in the New Kingdom (1550–1069 BCE), the festival
began with ritual seed sowing. The seeds were formed into the
shape of Osiris, and miniature seedbeds were laid down in troughs.

This focus on the beginning of the life cycle of grain was
mirrored in tomb rituals including forming the seedbeds, placing
little packets of earth in the tombs, and chanting spells to renew
the barley grain. On the preceding days, the festival included
watering the seedbeds, and the goddess Netjeryt tying strings of
onions. Similar ceremonies took place in temples across the land,
changing across time and place, but ending in the raising of the
Djed Pillar, the resurrection of Osiris, and a potent symbol of
Ma'at, as Djed means stability.

The rituals were elaborated by the Late Period (664–332 BCE).
Figures of Osiris and Sokar, a falcon-headed god of Memphis, were
fashioned from soil and seeds and in every temple in the city were

OPPOSITE: **An otherwise
timeless image of a field
near the Nile shows
a motorized pump
replacing a shaduf to
irrigate the wheat.**

RIGHT: At Khoiak, models of silt and seeds were pressed into Osiris-shaped moulds. When planted and watered, they sprouted.

BELOW: Shu and Tefnut protect this important Menat ritual instrument, which held a beaded collar rattle, an Usekh.

buried in the earth, the seeds embedded in them frozen in time. The figures from the previous year were unearthed to complete the cycle of renewal. Evidence for this Khoiak festival has been recently discovered at Karnak.

Celebrating with music and dance

At celebrations of all kinds, dancers and singers performed to the rhythm of drums, bone clappers, tambourines and cymbals. Tunes were played on harps and lutes. Dancing was expressive, often performed with sweeping, gyrating movements, pirouettes and leaps. Dances were performed not only at festivals but also at banquets. Some styles were combative movements, symbolizing battle, while others were sombre dances performed by *mutu*, a specialist funerary troupe dressed in kilts and crowns made of reeds. The god Osiris and his wife Isis grew in strength through the dynasties, and dances were demanded of those who celebrated these deities in the many festivals held for them throughout the year.

Tekh festival, when Re changes heart

Around the Middle Kingdom, a festival emerged from a story woven around the gentle, fun-loving goddess, Hathor, also known as the Lady of Inebriation. It celebrates the time when

overindulging on beer saved humankind from annihilation at
the hand of a wrathful Re. For his part, Re watched earthlings as
they squabbled and fought, and in exasperation at their cruelty
decided to teach them a lesson, through Hathor's feline aspect.

Re sent the fearsome wildcat goddess Sekhmet to murder
them, which she did by ripping them to shreds and gulping down
their blood. Re looked on the carnage unfolding before his eyes
and thought with satisfaction how well Sekhmet was applying
herself. That was until other deities asked him how earthlings
would learn a lesson if Sekhmet murdered them all.

Re, feeling perturbed, turned to a surprising deity to save
the situation. Tenenet, the goddess of beer and merriment, was
tasked to dye a batch of beer with pomegranate juice so that
it looked like blood, and transported it to Dendera, where
Sekhmet was ploughing a path of carnage and chaos.
Spying the fake blood, the ever-thirsty Sekhmet stopped in
her tracks, drank all the beer and fell fast asleep, waking
later and miraculously as the benign, generous and fun-
loving Hathor.

The Tekh festival, like many, rose and fell over the next
millennia, reviving in the Roman period (30 BCE–395 CE),
and involving much drinking and drumming to facilitate
close communion with the goddess. Hathor, linked at times
with Mut, another great sky goddess and mother figure, saw
her festival transferred to Mut's temples, with evidence of
celebratory rituals depicted at her temple at Karnak in a
space devoted to drunkenness.

Hathor, and goddesses with whom she melded, became
renowned for their fun-loving influence at other festivals
and family gatherings, not to mention their endorsement of
free-flowing beer. Hathor's own festival, which predates the
Tekh festival, was very similar to it. Based largely at her cult
centre at Dendera, this celebration of family gatherings, feasting,
drinking, dancing and singing aimed also to enable better,
less inhibited communication with the goddess, and became
popular in temples outside her main influence. Despite all
this merriment, a little caution was required, for Hathor had a
hidden, darker side whose name was Sekhmet.

BELOW: Sekhmet wears
a sun disc and uraeus
crown; and holds a
papyrus sceptre and
the ankh of life.

ABOVE: Rameses II, with Thoth behind him, honours the Theban triad of Amun, Mut and Khonsu at the Ramesseum Temple, Luxor.

Festivals of beauty

It is hard to imagine a festival that was arranged to include all Ancient Egyptians in such a stratified society. But from the Middle Kingdom (2055–1650 BCE), a celebration of Amun, Mut and Khonsu was one of these, taking place between Harvest Tide and New Year. This was Wadi Festival, also known as the Beautiful Feast of the Valley. Simultaneously a festival to honour Amun, Mut and Khonsu, and the dead of all classes in society, it has echoes of All Saints, All Souls and Hallowe'en, which were initially a cluster of sun cult festivals that were subsequently adopted by Christianity.

In Ancient Egypt, statues of the gods were paraded from their temples and across the river to the necropolis, with Amun sailing from Karnak to Thebes. At the same time, ordinary folk took flowers, food and drink as offerings to their deceased loved ones buried in more modest graveyards, carrying likenesses of dead souls along the way. Remembering that images for Ancient Egyptians were seen as the embodiment of the actual person or god represented, this was a poignant and powerful ceremony.

The Wag festival was dedicated not only to the death of Osiris but also to those of family members across the land. Miniature boats made from papyrus paper were placed on graves, facing west towards the setting sun and the great abyss of the desert, and papyrus votive shrines were floated on the Nile.

Neith, goddess of the cosmos, was the focus of a simple but beautiful festival in her honour, when, all over Egypt, people came out of their houses and lit oil lamps that shone like stars, linking earth with the heavens and ensuring that the balance of Ma'at was maintained.

The powerful bull cult

The power of the bull god, whose most famous form was Apis, goes back to predynastic times. It was associated with the first kings, who were depicted in bull form or associated with the power of bulls on ceremonial artworks such as the Narmer Palette.

Apis, a royal sacred bull, was picked out for his special markings and treated to the best shelter, food, medical treatment, and a bevy of beautiful cows to keep him company. A ceremonial mummification and burial in a granite coffin marked his death, which saw crowds of mourners lining the route from his cult centre at Memphis to a dedicated Apis necropolis, the Serapeum. According to the Greek historian Herodotus (482–425 BCE), the chosen bull needed to be: 'black with a white diamond on his forehead, the image of a vulture on its back, a scarab-shaped mark under its tongue and double hairs on its tail'.

Every year, in a seven-day bull festival, Apis was led along streets lined with cheering crowds; the children pushed forward, so that if they drew in the bull's breath they would be granted the gift of clairvoyance.

BELOW: Apis is honoured on a painted limestone stela from the Memphis Serapeum dedicated to deceased Apis bulls.

The Raising of the Heavens

Auspicious times of the year, particularly solstices and half points, have been marked as occasions when gods appear and are celebrated in cultures all over the world. In Ancient Egypt, the Midwinter Festival of the sun god, Amun, or Amun-Re, was one such occasion, occurring at the sixth month of their calendar year. Often referred to as the great Raising of the Heavens, this celebrated the creation myth in which the earth and the heavens were separated by the trunk of the Ished tree, also known as the Tree of Life.

On this auspicious day, temple workers at Iunu collected branches of the persea, the sycamore, the acacia or the willow, in honour of the god and the tree itself. Its fruits, when eaten, gave eternal life and all knowledge of time, which was pertinent to marking the halfway point of the year. The day following the festival, the first of the seventh month of the year, a ceremony took place for 'filling in' the sacred eye of Re at Iunu.

According to an entry in a diary belonging to a builder at Deyr al-Medinah's workmen's village, around the time of the Midwinter Festival for Amun, another celebration took

BELOW: *Procession of the Sacred Bull Apis* by Frederick Arthur (1847–1928) shows adoration for Apis, who became Osiris-Apis at death.

place, this time for Ptah, creator god and god of carpenters and construction workers. This festival was clearly important for the builder, who was beginning work on the king's tomb.

Yet for most of the villagers, in the dusty, snake- and scorpion-infested desert, it was a snake deity who was the most favoured. This could well have been the cobra goddess Renenutet.

Renenutet, the cobra goddess of contrasts

A festival took place for Renenutet at the eight or ninth month of the year. Her name, meaning 'she who rears', well described this cobra goddess from the Nile Delta. As a nurturing goddess, she is seen as a mother figure, yet was also known to kill with her gaze. Her festival occurred at harvest time, when snakes were rampant in the barley and wheat fields, waiting for the hordes of rodents escaping the scythe. For Renenutet's help in catching the rats, and to protect themselves against her venom, farmers made offerings of grain, and built shrines around breweries and wineries. Renenutet's was one of many festivals for harvest time, when gratitude and hope abounded, and when tired farmers could look forward to a time of rest.

Between predynastic and Roman times, the main festivals changed to include newly ascending gods and goddesses. Festivals came and went, although some continued long beyond the time of Ancient Egypt. What did not come and go, was death.

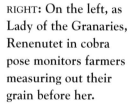

RIGHT: On the left, as Lady of the Granaries, Renenutet in cobra pose monitors farmers measuring out their grain before her.

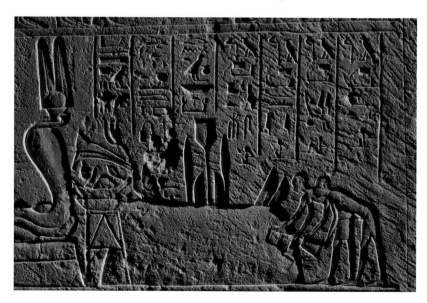

Gods and priests of the mortuary temple

When Osiris was murdered by his jealous brother Set, it was
Osiris's son Horus who opened the mouth of his deceased father,
enabling him to speak once more; to eat, drink, and to smile – if
we can imagine that gods enjoyed the lighter side of life. In short,
Horus gave his father the first earthly functions of existence after
death. In this way, Horus was born of Isis and his deceased father
Osiris, and he was guarded like a precious jewel by other gods.

It followed that the kings of Egypt, who were the
manifestations of Horus on earth, should also be granted an open
mouth so that they too could see on their journey through the
underworld and eat good food, drink fine wine and generally
enjoy life when they reached the heavenly Field of Reeds. More
importantly, an open mouth allowed the flow of the *ka* and other
vital spirits and parts of the soul. Over time, the opening of the
mouth was a privilege shared by viziers and other top officials,
high priests, people of wealth, the statues of all these people,
cult gods and goddesses, great structures such as temples, and the
revered sacred Apis Bull.

ABOVE: No deceased
person would pass
through the underworld
on a celestial boat
without facing an
Opening of the
Mouth ceremony.

GODS WHO OPENED THE MOUTHS OF THE DEAD

'I have opened your mouth, I have opened your two eyes. I have opened your mouth with the instrument of Anubis.'

This is a typical quote on the role of Anubis, who is often depicted as a main god of 'Opening the Mouth'. But the Papyrus of Ani (written by a scribe who lived between 1292 and 1188 BCE) shows us that many others, including the great sky gods, were involved. The procedure was not only about allowing the deceased to function as if he or she were alive, but also to allow the flow of the *ka* and other spiritual elements of the person.

'My mouth is opened by Ptah and what was on my mouth has been loosened by my local god. Thoth comes indeed, filled and equipped with magic, and the bonds of Set, which restricted my mouth, have been loosened. Atum has warded them off and has cast away the restrictions of Set. My mouth is opened, my mouth is split open by Shu with that iron harpoon of his with which he split open the mouths of the gods.'

From The Papyrus of Ani, on opening the mouth of Osiris, translator: E. A. Wallis Budge.

The 'Opening of the Mouth' ceremony was granted to several gods including two sharp-faced deities: Sokar and Anubis, the black jackal-headed god whose colour represented the positive fertile Nile silt and the more negative decayed corpse. In these roles, which represented the earth in which new life would rise and the dark state of death, Anubis became the mummifier of the body, preserving it for resurrection. Yet he is also the god who is often depicted holding the scales that weighed the heart against Ma'at's white feather of justice; a nervous moment for the deceased.

Anubis's commitment to his corpses and the *ka* souls within them was inherited by the next generation in his daughter, Kabechet, who calmed the soul in its hour of judgement in the Hall of Truth with cooling water and a promise to be one of the guides along the hard path to eternity.

Sekhmet, goddess of healers

Was she a lioness with a red skirt that represented a lust for blood, or a protective wildcat goddess who wore red to symbolize the gentle setting sun? Like most gods and goddesses, the fierce warrior Sekhmet had a contrasting, softer side, which in her case was as a healer and the protector of all healers and medicine makers. As the Red Lady symbolizing the parched red desert sand, she could be seen as the champion of all those who faced harsh times of whatever kind, and for which, in Ancient Egypt, a magic formula, a doctor's potion, or an oracle could be found to alleviate the pain.

Together with Heka, an ancient predynastic sky god seen as an aspect of the sun god Re, and one of magic and medicine, Sekhmet healed both the living and the dead. Heka, an ethereal god who until the Late Period had no temple or shrine to his name, was mentioned in medical texts and inscriptions for magic spells and chants. Heka was one of the most mystical of mythical beings, with no great stories to his name. But his intangible magic force was considered essential in creating the world at the beginning of time.

Sem priests presided over the rituals of death, from incantations to performing aspects of mummification, and, crucially, chanting the spells that would send the deceased on a safe journey through to a blissful afterlife. A *sem* priest would have his own specialization, and while those who recited sacred texts were revered, others who performed the cutting of the corpse were rather reviled. Possibly this had something to do with the fearsome and rather unattractive jackal-headed Anubis. Whatever the reason, this hapless *sem* priest was ritually verbally abused and chased down the street.

Prising open the mouth

Sokar, god of agriculture, of death, the necropolis, coffin building, and many other mysteries and crafts, is also accredited by some as the god of the 'Opening of the

OPPOSITE: **Royal falcon god Horus opens the mouth of Rameses II (1279–1213 BCE).**

BELOW: **Thutmose III (1479–1426 BCE) holds Heka's healing hand in Khnum's temple.**

Mouth' ceremony. Although his sharp, hawk-like head might make the process appear rather violent, it was thought for a long time that mortuary *sem* priests, led by Kher-heb, the lector priest, opened the mouth of the deceased with a reverential, gentle process, preceded by the ceremonial insertion of the lead priest's finger. That was until skulls were studied more closely, and it was discovered that the jaw was wrenched apart rather violently using knives, iron chisels or adzes and even the foreleg of a bull, which, though blessed by the lips of the priest, left broken teeth and fractured jaw bones.

This was probably not a procedure of choice. Texts such as the Apis Embalming Ritual demand that the corpse, once cut, eviscerated and dehydrated, required its mouth to be opened up again, wiped clean, anointed with scented and medicinal oils and swabbed with preserving resins.

By this time, rigor mortis would have set in, so the priests had little choice but to prise open the mouth. Once this procedure

BELOW: Sokar, as god of cemeteries, sails in a sacred boat adorned by the head of an oryx; a symbol of the murderous god, Set.

had been completed, the body could be wrapped with linen, resins and herbs, amulets bound in, and the fractured face covered with a beautiful painted mask. The Ancient Egyptian words for 'opening the mouth' included *wpi*, which describes the wrenching apart of two opposing forces, so the method used to respect the rules laid out in the text should not come as a surprise. Sokar, a god of many things, is celebrated at the Khoiak festival, in roles far removed from the dissecting table.

The god Horus was never far away from any situation, in life and in death. After evisceration, internal organs were placed in canopic jars that represented Horus's four children: jackal-headed Duamutef, ape-headed Hapi, human-headed Imsety and falcon-headed Qebehsenuef. Here, the body parts were well protected.

Priests and the gods and goddesses of medicine

Surgery on corpses certainly taught *sem* priests a lot about the body, and formed a basis for a canon of medical texts, many of which were stored in temple libraries: the Houses of Life. However, steeped as Ancient Egyptians were in the powers of deities, scientific knowledge on its own was never going to work. The healing strengths of Hathor and Sekhmet were nothing if not combined with the magic of Serket and Heka. Together, these gave Ancient Egyptians protection, relief from pain, and cure. It was the role of priests to combine magic and medicine, giving them more tangible roles as doctors and surgeons.

The name 'Sekhmet priests' was given to temple doctors and reveals the strength of belief in the gods to work for the good of humankind. Doctors as a separate body did exist, along with exorcists and consultants of oracles, who understood that through their stories, gods and goddesses had specialist powers.

For example, Bes, the demon god, protected and assisted pregnant women, babies and mothers in childbirth, and vulnerable infants. Serket, as goddess of healing, stings and bites, could alleviate the pain of scorpions, and counter the venom of snakes; both creatures so feared and so prevalent in the desert environment. Ta-Bitjet, a scorpion goddess, could preside over the use of scorpion blood as an antidote to all poisons.

These kinds of belief and practice were not necessarily followed in all parts of the kingdom, or throughout time, but the principles of prevention and cure through a combination of the power of the supernatural and the science of the day prevailed, as evinced in the Ebers papyrus.

The Ebers papyrus: a medical textbook

In 1873, Maurice Ebers, a German Egyptologist and novelist, bought a 20m-long (65ft) long papyrus treatise on how magic and

ABOVE: **Two of Horus's canopic jar 'children' show Imsety (top) guarding the liver and Duamutef shielding the stomach.**

medicine could work together to defy the diseases and injuries inflicted upon Ancient Egyptians by demons and spirits. Written during the reign of Amenophis I also known as Amenhotep I (c. 1514–1493), the Ebers medical dictionary contains 700 magic remedies with formulae.

The text shows us probably the most modern interpretation of illness that Ancient Egyptians ever experienced. Although it is not medicine as we know it, it shows insight into a range of problems, both physical and mental. Through this and other sources we know that surgical skills on surface wounds could be successfully undertaken, carefully sutured and treated with the antiseptic qualities of plants such as willow.

Many illnesses that we know today were identified. Although treatment was limited, it did not seem too harmful, and some medicinal substances have proven value. Asthma was treated with a mixture of honey, milk, sesame and frankincense, while stomach upsets were soothed with juniper, mint, garlic and sandalwood. Burns were eased with a lotion of aloe. The importance of cleanliness, although not analyzed, was well understood, and people were urged to wash every day, and to eat well but modestly.

Despite a detailed knowledge of the body, the arteries, veins, intestines and all other kinds of tubing were grouped together in a system of 46 channels called *metu*, which were all linked to the heart. These *metu* could become blocked by Wekhedu, an evil spirit, whose wicked work forced pus to the surface of the body – an affliction cured only by giving the patient an enema. This idea of ridding the body of its poisons and bad spirits was a central theory upon which much medicine was based.

Many Ancient Egyptians still sought preventions and cures outside the theories expounded in the Ebers papyrus. They included amulets, incense, offerings and

OPPOSITE: **Part of the Ebers Papyrus (c.1550 BCE), this 20m (65ft) tract gives about 900 medical diagnoses and prescriptions.**

BELOW: **A patient receives ophthalmic treatment on this reconstruction of a papyrus from the tomb of the vizier Ipi.**

tattoos, which appealed more to gods than doctors. In many respects, especially by the New Kingdom, Ancient Egypt did have a system of examination and treatment that we can recognize. It even had a healthcare plan for workers. But there was never any suggestion that medical knowledge on its own would suffice; nor that deities such as Isis, goddess of healing, magic and perfection, should be sidelined.

BELOW: **A cippi demonstrates infant Horus's power as he stands on a crocodile.**

THE PROTECTIVE CIPPI OF HORUS

Most Ancient Egyptians wore protective amulets against all sorts of illnesses and malevolent forces. There were also plaques, or cippi, that served the same purpose and resembled small round-topped stelae. On one side, a carved relief figure of Horus as a child showed him standing on crocodiles and holding the most threatening creatures of the desert: snakes, scorpions and lions. These plaques were produced quite late in Ancient

Egypt's history, up to the Ptolemaic era (332–30 BCE), showing the enduring power of the gods in preventing harm.

Larger plaques were engraved with hymns, spells and incantations that called upon Horus to protect both people and, sometimes, other gods. The 'magic of Heka' in the spells was only released when water poured over the cippus was drunk by the afflicted. The following spell forms part of a plea from the great god, Thoth.

Hail Horus emerged from Osiris, born of Isis the goddess,
I have spoken with your name,
I have recited from your words of power…
… It is your formulae which come from your mouth,
commanded for you by your father Geb
given to you by your mother Nut,
taught by your brother Khentykem
to make your guard, to repeat your protection,
to seal the mouth of every serpent of those in the sky,
those on the land, those in the water…
to make people live, to make the gods content
(Source unproven)

Priests as narrators of myths and guardians of history

We have a lot to thank Ancient Egypt's priests for in their conscientious studies and gift to humankind of the concept of the library. It is largely through them that we can study the myths of the gods in the spells and hymns that they incanted, wrote down and preserved.

On their own, the vast quantities of inscriptions, texts, artefacts, friezes, monuments, temples and pyramids provide a lot of information about myths, the pantheon and divine kingship. Archaeologists can use modern scientific methods to date them. But it is thanks largely to Manetho, an Egyptian priest and historian from the third century BCE, that we can also chart these changes and put names and narratives of kings, gods and their myths to images and dates of archaeological finds.

In his timeline of Ancient Egyptian history, Manetho identified 30 consecutive dynasties, with named rulers, across three Kingdoms: Old, Middle and New. He also included disruptive hiatuses between the Kingdoms: the Intermediate Periods. During these times of political realignment, great changes in the hierarchy of gods and their accompanying myths often occurred. Manetho, aware of the power throughout Egypt's history of its belief system, also wove gods and the divinity of kings into Ancient Egypt's narrative, through stable and unstable times.

Manetho's work, written in Greek, was commissioned by the Ancient Greek ruler Ptolemy II Philadephus (285–246 BCE). To compile it, Manetho researched oral traditions, written histories and other king lists such as the Turin Papyrus of Kings, produced in hieratic script from around 1292–1190 BCE. He also

BELOW: **Papyri at Turin's Egyptian Museum include this geological map of gold and silver mining operations in the Eastern Desert.**

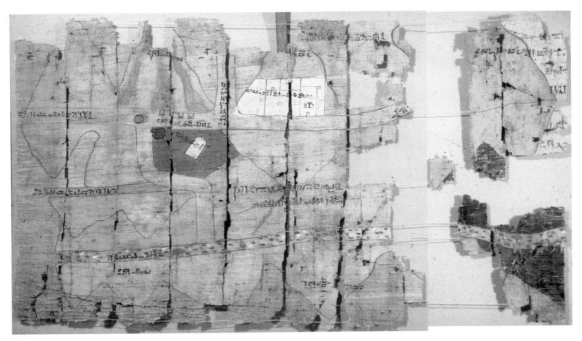

wove into the narrative certain gods and divine kings. Although a copy of Manetho's work has never been found in its entirety, fragments have surfaced. These have been used by other scholars as the basis for reconstructing a comprehensive king list.

Bringing Ancient Egypt into the light

One of the scholars who used Manetho's work in constructing his own timeline, which is known simply as *Chronicle*, was Eusebius (c. 260–339 CE), a Christian historian and theologian from Palestine, who referenced the influence of Ethiopia, Persia and Macedonia at certain times in his timeline.

Sextus Julius Africanus (180–250 CE), a scholar and Christian historian from Jerusalem, tried in his *Chronographiai* (221 CE) to date the dynasties by setting the list against events in the Bible and the timeline of another ancient civilization, the Chaldaean (tenth to sixth centuries BCE) from southern Babylonia (modern-day southern Iraq).

It is now thought that these and other histories were probably somewhat skewed by political pressures put upon the authors of the time to promote some civilizations above others. But their inclusion in Ancient Egypt's narrative of kingship and myth makes us aware that there existed parallel mythologies, belief systems and cultural structures in other parts of the world.

Ancient Egypt's myths have changed over time, and gods and goddesses have risen and fallen in favour with individual rulers or entire dynasties. Without a historical timeline to pin dates to known periods and rulers, scholars would have found difficulty in assessing their relevance or establishing pivotal points of change.

Priests and gods in times of change

The path of gods, goddesses, their myths and the priests who served them was not a smooth one throughout the history of Ancient Egypt. During the Intermediate Periods, kings and queens were not necessarily fully in charge; capital cities moved; cult gods and goddesses rose and fell in power. Priests were sometimes winners and at other times losers. During the reign of Akhenaten (1351–1336 BCE), the majority of great gods and goddesses were sidelined in favour of one supreme god, Aten.

The fate of priests for other cult deities hung in the balance. Weaving in and out of these changes were others, such as exploration, trade, warfare and invasion, that had an equally profound effect on gods and goddesses and their priests, bringing ideas and practices from belief systems outside the kingdom, and spreading Ancient Egypt's pantheon far beyond its boundaries.

ABOVE: Eusebius, Bishop of Caesarea, also wrote about Egypt's many 'gods, demi-gods and shades,' meaning spirits of the dead.

6

TRADE, INVASION, EXPANSION AND MYTH

Changes to the aspects of gods, goddesses and their myths over thousands of years were at times processes of evolution, often inspired by the preferences of kings or the pressures on their reign. At other times, they occurred as a result of influences from other lands and civilizations, through trade, warfare, invasion and expansion.

Shu, god of emptiness and the arid desert, was also the god of light in the darkness and of cool air, and could overcome the danger of snakes. Shu would be the god of choice when travelling across the Sahara or hoping for a fresh breeze to fill a barque's sails on the open seas. His versatility for an Ancient Egyptian trader was useful, for there were deals to be made with nations

OPPOSITE: Amenhotep IV (1359–1336 BCE) changed his name to Akhenaten and upset the entire pantheon during his reign.

that could only be reached after perilous journeys over dry, barren landscapes and mountains, along rivers, and across the Mediterranean, with the unpredictable life-threatening storms that made it so perilous.

From predynastic times, traders looked as far south as Nubia and Sudan, eastward to Arabia and Mesopotamia, and west to Libya and beyond. Ships and donkey trains stopped at trading cities sprinkled along the Mediterranean coastline of the Near East in a region called the Levant, where Syria, Lebanon, Palestine and Israel now lie. Ancient Egypt's merchants moved goods up and down these margins of the great Asian continent, and around the islands that dotted the sea between Africa and Europe.

It was inevitable that cultural exchange should occur and that belief systems should form a large slice of this – especially since

RIGHT: **Traders bartered along the Mediterranean and beyond, exchanging gods as well as goods.**

Ancient Egypt's urge to trade was created in part by the demand for luxury goods to furnish temples to the gods, adorn their statues, and lavishly decorate pyramids and palaces of divine kings.

For these purposes, Egypt, the breadbasket of Africa at that time, exported wheat and barley, gold, leather, papyrus for papermaking and linen made from the flax that was cultivated abundantly along the River Nile. In exchange, she received woods such as cedar and ebony; ivory; lapis lazuli and other semi-precious and precious stones; perfumed oils and resins (frankincense and myrrh among them); silver, copper, iron, and even cattle, to supplement Egypt's herds.

While trade for these luxury goods was often carried out peaceably, force was sometimes used. Even early dynastic rulers such as King Djer (3050–3000 BCE) made incursions south into Nubia, where he secured fortified trading posts from which to despatch gold, ivory and woods unobtainable from Lebanon, the main source of the cedarwood that was used so widely.

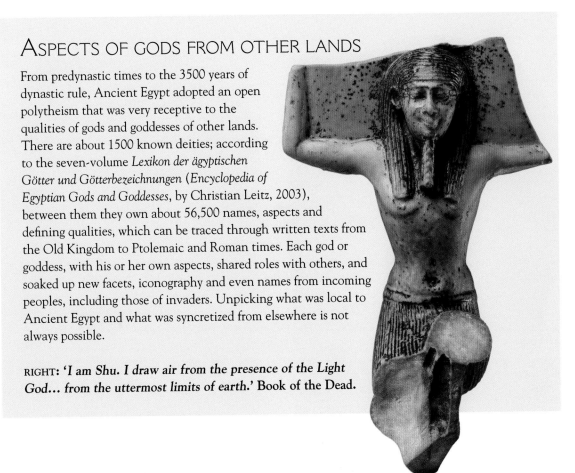

ASPECTS OF GODS FROM OTHER LANDS

From predynastic times to the 3500 years of dynastic rule, Ancient Egypt adopted an open polytheism that was very receptive to the qualities of gods and goddesses of other lands. There are about 1500 known deities; according to the seven-volume *Lexikon der ägyptischen Götter und Götterbezeichnungen* (*Encyclopedia of Egyptian Gods and Goddesses*, by Christian Leitz, 2003), between them they own about 56,500 names, aspects and defining qualities, which can be traced through written texts from the Old Kingdom to Ptolemaic and Roman times. Each god or goddess, with his or her own aspects, shared roles with others, and soaked up new facets, iconography and even names from incoming peoples, including those of invaders. Unpicking what was local to Ancient Egypt and what was syncretized from elsewhere is not always possible.

RIGHT: *'I am Shu. I draw air from the presence of the Light God... from the uttermost limits of earth.'* Book of the Dead.

Gods and goddesses from far away

The name 'Mesopotamia', an area covering ancient Iraq, means the 'land between two rivers': the Tigris and Euphrates. These great arteries not only watered a prime agricultural region – the Fertile Crescent – but also provided the highways for trading vessels to the Gulf. From at least the Old Kingdom (2686–2160 BCE), Ancient Egypt interacted with the great states that emerged from this region: Sumer, Babylonia and Assyria were probably the most influential in economic, military and cultural terms.

From at least 5000 BCE, Sumerian traders and those from prominent towns on the Nile Delta exchanged goods and, it is thought, cultural ideas and artforms, especially related to their belief systems. The two kingdoms shared similar categories of gods and goddesses: the cosmic and the anthropomorphic; the protective and the warlike; and those who represented natural forces or intellectual powers such as knowledge of astronomy, magic and justice. Therefore, the chances of gods and goddesses travelling happily between these territories were high.

BELOW: Kadesh on her sacred lion, faces deathly Reshef (left). On a statue to Astarte, goddess Roma protects Rome (right).

From Old Kingdom pyramid texts we can see some gods and goddesses appearing from other lands, such as Dedwen, a lion god and provider of royal incense from Nubia, Ancient Egypt's southern neighbour. By the New Kingdom (1550–1069 BCE), gods and goddesses from the Near and Middle East, such as Anat, Astarte, Hauron, Reshef, Kadesh and Baal, were worshipped widely: some took on aspects previously seen only as the privilege of the most ancient Egyptian gods. Yam, a god from the Levant, became a deity of the sea, which perpetuated his links between the two lands that he served.

By the Late Period (664–332 BCE) and into the Ptolemaic era (332–30 BCE), key local gods and those from other kingdoms were sometimes fused together, such as Anat-Hathor, a combination of a goddess from the Levant and the timeless Hathor. Towards the end of Ancient Egypt's long history, there was a great melding of gods, so that Egypt's Osiris and Apis fused

ANCIENT EGYPT'S MYTHOLOGY AND OUTSIDE INFLUENCE

The Gebel el-Arak knife, dated between about 3400 and 3000 BCE, and the ceremonial Narmer Palette of the same period are two principal Ancient Egyptian artefacts purported to demonstrate the influence of the Sumerians of Mesopotamia. The ivory knife handle is carved with a ferocious naval battle scene depicting, it is said, Sumerian fighters, who are succumbing to bearded Egyptians. On the other side, a Sumerian king, with his shepherd's crown, is surrounded by animals, from lions to rams, which symbolized his identity as Master of Nature. Sumer's influence on the Narmer Palette is seen largely as artistic, apart from the two great serpents depicted on one side; these have been associated with Ningishzida, a god of the underworld, whose symbol was the serpent, and Basmu, 'Lord of the Good Tree', a protector and god of fertility.

That artistic styles and symbols travel far is indisputable. But using these isolated pieces of evidence as examples of a greater influence on Ancient Egypt's mythology, as some historians have done, belies the strength of its belief system. In terms of serpents and serpent gods, Ancient Egypt (and Africa as a whole) had had their own for many millennia.

RIGHT: **The Gebel el-Arak knife blade is made of high quality ocher slate, attached to a hippopotamus tooth handle.**

ABOVE: **A black diorite statue, dedicated to god Ningishzida, shows Gudea, King of Mesopotamian city-state, Lagash.**

with the Greek Zeus, king of the gods, and Bacchus, the god of wine, to become the Ptolemaic Serapis.

Gods, myths and priests from incomers and conquerors

As Ancient Egypt flourished, immigrants were drawn to the kingdom from far and wide for work opportunities or to join mercenary units of armies, both regional and national. It is inevitable that they brought with them their own cultures, belief systems, gods and myths. Invaders, from the Hittites whose empire rested between the Mediterranean and the Black Sea in the north, where Turkey now lies, to Nubians in the south, Libyans to the west, Persians from the Euphrates region, and the mysterious Hyksos from who knows where (perhaps Palestine), brought not only gods and myths but also ideas that they too could enter the powerful priesthood. Often, their way was opened up by schisms between Upper and Lower Egypt, and between pivotal cities such as Memphis and Thebes, empowered by their cult gods and goddesses.

Priest kings from Libya

To the consternation of Ma'at, the god of harmony, Ancient Egypt had few periods during which a single king or queen ruled both Upper and Lower Egypt in peace and tranquillity. The term 'Intermediate' is used by historians to explain periods that followed the beginnings of powerful social change in Ancient Egypt, or times of turmoil, of which neighbouring nations often took advantage, making changes to religious institutions as well as political ones.

One such period followed the rule of Rameses XI (1102–1073 BCE or 1069 BCE), whose reign began with civil unrest and rampant tomb robbing. Amenhotep, the High Priest of Amun at Thebes, had become so powerful that Rameses hired Nubian troops under the command of Viceroy Pinehesy to oust him. Yet chaos continued. In a desperate bid to secure some kind of control, Rameses placed military leaders as state governors in both Upper and Lower Egypt. In Upper Egypt, he installed Piankh and Herihor, who had risen from the ranks of a

previously invading Libyan army. Historians wrangle over which of these two took control first, but it is Herihor who became the most renowned.

Not content with being a regional governor, Herihor took over as High Priest of Amun and became a second king to Rameses. The power of the gods was such, however, that his status as high priest gave him the upper hand. It was he who interceded between the gods and humankind as a lordly god himself. He took on the trappings of a divine king, including a divine queen, Nodjmet. Together, they appear in papyrus texts praising and adoring the god Osiris, who would doubtless see them through to a heavenly afterlife with all the other kings and queens. Herihor's grandiose ideas knew no bounds. On the walls of the Karnak temple complex, he can be seen wearing the double crown of Upper and Lower Egypt, and his name is inscribed within the royal cartouche.

ABOVE: **Herihor, as king, faces Horus, in Karnak Temple.**

BELOW: **Queen Nodjmet's mummy was embalmed with her heart still in place inside her body.**

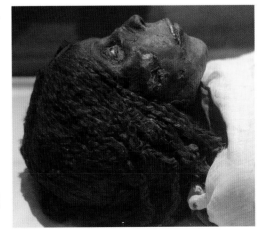

Herihor is just one example of a person with political ambitions whose origins lay outside Ancient Egypt and who arose within the religious hierarchy, jolting perceptions of a homegrown belief system. But influence went both ways, and in equal measure.

During the heyday of the New Kingdom (1550–1069 BCE), Ancient Egypt flourished, its economy boomed, and rulers sought to expand its boundaries, creating an empire that ran through much of the Levant, from Sinai in the south, through Canaan and into Syria as far as the border with Cilicia in the north, which created a buffer zone between Egypt and the Hittite Empire in what is now Turkey. The flurry of exchange of all kinds was set to increase, and included not only individual deities but also religious concepts, artforms, insignia and the narrative of myths.

BELOW: **Pharaohs with a sacred tree under a winged sun disc and uraei are carved on an ivory from Nimrud city, Assyria.**

Travelling images from Ancient Egypt

It is thought that even during the Old Kingdom, Egyptian iconography, divine kingship, and the name of the god Osiris reached Mesopotamia. Ivory images of Egyptian gods can be found on Assyrian furniture and appear as protective symbols on horses' tackle and on amulets. During the Middle Kingdom (2055–1650 BCE), symbols and icons of several Egyptian deities began to appear in the Near East and Anatolia (modern Turkey). The image of Narmer, the mythical king who united Upper and Lower Egypt, smiting his enemies, was adapted in the Levant to empower Baal, their winged god of storms and fertile soil, in a similar pose, holding a lightning bolt. Other images, such as the winged solar disc, the sphinx and the ankh symbol of life, became part of the Near East's visual library, while it is thought by some historians that Egypt's growing influence on the Middle East inspired some of the symbolism in the biblical world.

The power of Ancient Egypt's myths beyond its borders

Khonsu, whose name means 'the one who travels', was a great god of the moon, which, by the grace of the god, charts its course across the skies. His role as protector of wanderers and travellers gave him a solid following in a land where trade, exploration and military campaigns were the foundation of the rise and expansion of Ancient Egypt. Khonsu's responsibilities were not confined to protecting the journeys of earthlings. As messenger to the gods, his role was pivotal in restoring Ma'at, or harmony, in the cosmos and on earth.

ABOVE: Khonsu, once said to be a devourer of dead kings' hearts, as a Theban aspect, became a god who decides life span.

The following myth, which was probably written in the time of Rameses II (1279–1213 BCE) – though some say it was Rameses III (1187–1156 BCE) – puts Khonsu centre-stage in a narrative that demonstrates Ancient Egypt's power and influence outside its own borders. His aspects evolved down the ages, and his parentage changed too, but he, along with his associate, Thoth, always championed the traveller. In a grey granite statue uncovered at Karnak, he holds a triple-headed sceptre representing life, prosperity and stability, all maintained by the constant cycle of the moon.

Rameses and the Princess of Bekhten

King Rameses travelled far with a great entourage to the country of Nehern in western Syria near the River Euphrates.

He journeyed here every year to gather taxes and gifts from the chiefs of lands over which he held suzerainty. Rameses, guided by the great moon god Khonsu, travelled to all corners, even as far as the dangerous terrain of the mighty swamps. Wherever he went, chiefs came bearing great gifts to the Souls of His Majesty. They included gold, lapis lazuli, turquoise, and planks of wood of every kind, all carried on the backs of their pack animals, and each chief's tribute was more precious and heavier than that of his neighbour.

One chief, the Prince of Bekhten, brought some of the most valuable gifts of all, at the head of which was his eldest daughter, Re-Neferu. The prince lavished praise upon Rameses and asked for his clemency in all things, especially pleading that the king take his daughter as a gift. Now Rameses thought that the princess was the loveliest woman in the world, so he accepted her as his bride and wrote down her new title: Great Royal Wife, Re-Neferu. Back in Egypt, he treated her in all the right ways, just as a Royal Wife would expect.

Then, in the second month of the harvest season of *shemu* in the fifteenth year of his reign, Rameses journeyed to Thebes, the Mighty Mistress of Cities, to give thanks to the great god Amun for his bounty. There, at the seat of the heart of the god, the spot chosen since primeval times, Rameses was taking

ABOVE: **At Karnak, Khonsu Temple's Peristyle Court is decorated with a relief of sacred uraei, indicating Khonsu's power.**

part in the beautiful harvest ceremonies of the Festival of the Southern Apt when an emissary arrived from Bekhten.

Rameses graciously received the emissary and accepted the gifts sent for the Royal Wife by her father. But the Prince of Bekhten had a separate agenda. The emissary, prostrating himself before Rameses, pleaded, 'Praise be to you, Sun Re of the Nine Nations of the Bow. We beg you for mercy, for Prince Bekhten's second daughter, Bent-Reshet, has fallen so ill that it has affected her whole body, and it is feared she will die. The prince pleads with you, Your Majesty, to send a man of learning to see her.'

Rameses sent for his magician scribes from the House of Life, together with the palace nobles. He explained the situation to them and asked that the one with the wisest heart and the deftest fingers be brought before them. So the royal scribe, Tehuti-em-Heb, came forward and Rameses ordered him to depart to Bekhten with an ambassador. When he got there, Tehuti-em-Heb found that Bent-Reshet was possessed by an evil spirit, and would not respond to him.

So the Prince of Bekhten sent another emissary to Rameses, saying, 'Oh King, my Lord, I pray to you to send a god to banish the spirit, for only a god will have the power.' It was another auspicious time of the year, so Rameses went to the temple of the moon god, Khonsu Nefer-hetep, knowing that as a god of travel he would be perfect for the task.

'Oh my gracious Lord, I come to implore you once more on behalf of the dying daughter of Prince Bekhten.'

The great god Khonsu imbued a fine statue with his magic powers and sent his likeness, which was a true embodiment of himself, with the emissary back to Bekhten. Khonsu's likeness and an entourage rode in chariots for 17 long months, but as soon as the god arrived in Bekhten he confronted the demon, exorcising his spirit from Princess Bent-Reshet, and curing her instantly.

INFLUENCES ON ART IN MYTH

The iconic, powerful pose of Narmer, the first semi-mythical king of a united Upper and Lower Egypt, as he smites his foes, spread to images of other gods within trading distance. These included a stele depicting Baal, the tempestuous storm god of the Levant, now housed in the Louvre. The side profile style common to most depictions of Ancient Egypt's gods and goddesses, with notable exceptions such as the mischievous sprite-god Bes, was also repeated. The ankh (the symbol of life for Ancient Egyptians), the sphinx, and the winged solar disc found their way into the iconography of the Near East and some parts of the Middle East. There is a certain synchronicity between the concepts and imagery of Ancient Egypt's belief system, especially during the New Kingdom, and those areas that became biblical lands.

RIGHT: A Syrian gilded and silver-plated Baal figurine (c. 1300 BCE) in Narmer pose, aiming a missing weapon.

OPPOSITE: Greek god Oedipus answered the riddle of the Sphinx, who, distraught, threw herself into the sea.

The demon, cowed and ashamed, asked Khonsu for his forgiveness and to feast with him as a sign of reconciliation before he left Bekhten forever. So they feasted together and the demon departed for his own realm. Khonsu, too, was keen to return home, but the Prince of Bekhten wanted to keep the god's power in his own land, and so held on to his likeness.

After three years, Khonsu was so desperate to return to Egypt that he transformed into a golden hawk and flew directly there, leaving the Prince ashamed of himself for holding the god for so long. The Prince, anxious to make amends, gathered together all the god's adornments and paraphernalia, added lavish gifts and loaded Khonsu's chariot, ready for the journey. The priest, Tehuti-em-Heb, the envoy and the entourage all went to Khonsu's home. Rameses, in respect for Khonsu, set his likeness in the Great Temple and laid the Prince of Bekhten's gifts around him as offerings. Rameses had done the right thing. The harmony required by Ma'at was restored, and all was right with the world.

BELOW: The Naxos Sphinx was erected on top of an Ionic column at Apollo's sanctuary at Delphi c. 560–570 BCE.

The sphinx beyond Egypt

Ancient Egypt's sphinx, once buried in sand on the Giza Plateau and now standing tall by the pyramids, is a mystery. Clearly revered, its original purpose is still a puzzle, though as it faces due east it became worshipped as Hor-em-Akhet, 'Horus of the Horizon' and therefore linked with the sun god, Re.

It is an ambiguous mix of human and beast, and as such fits well with one idea of its role in myth as a divine being who challenges others with puzzles and riddles. From at least the end of the Old Kingdom, in about 2160 BCE, its imagery spread from Egypt as far as Asia, where most expressions of it were female. But it is in Greece that the sphinx really took off from about 1600 BCE: quite literally, as after a while the creature grew wings. This, its best-known form, evolved in Boeotian Thebes, a city in central Greece, where a great legend grew around it.

A sphinx myth from Greece

The Muses were the nine creative and adored daughters of Zeus, the king of the gods. It was these imaginative goddesses who taught the winged sphinx a riddle. She was so pleased with its complexity that she set out to challenge her subjects with it. Now, the sphinx was a very hungry being, so decided that if people could not answer the riddle, she would chew them up.

Her question was: 'What creature has four legs, then two, then three, yet uses only one voice?' One by one the people failed to give the right answer. That was until Oedipus, the tragic king of

THE GREAT SPHINX OF GIZA

Measuring 20m (65ft) high and 73.5m (240ft) long, the Great Sphinx of Giza is the largest and best-known image of this cult figure, with its body of a lion and head of a king, or maybe queen. No one knows in whose image this great limestone edifice was carved, though it is likely to be from the Fourth Dynasty, and was probably commissioned by the sons of Khufu to honour him.

Its limestone construction has made it vulnerable to weathering, although this does not explain the severed nose, uraeus (the emblem on the headdress) and beard. There have been many theories around their absence, including a now debunked idea that Napoleon's troops blasted it off with a cannon. Could it have been an act of iconoclasm by Akhenaten, who famously destroyed temples and statues of gods other than Aten, whom he worshipped in an extreme monotheistic manner?

Thebes who had accidentally killed his father and unknowingly married his mother, turned up and gave her the answer,

'The creature you are referring to is the human being. First, he or she crawls on all fours, then walks on two legs. In old age, the two legs are frail, so the human being needs a third leg: a stick.'

The myth is mischievous and creative, but its characterization of the sphinx as a rather cruel and manipulative being is in stark contrast to the enduring reverence that Ancient Egyptians showed towards this powerful icon. The image of the sphinx travelled a long way, but its spirit clearly did not. This was

BELOW: The Great Sphinx is the largest unearthed across Luxor so far. A new sphinx discovered in 2018 is currently being excavated.

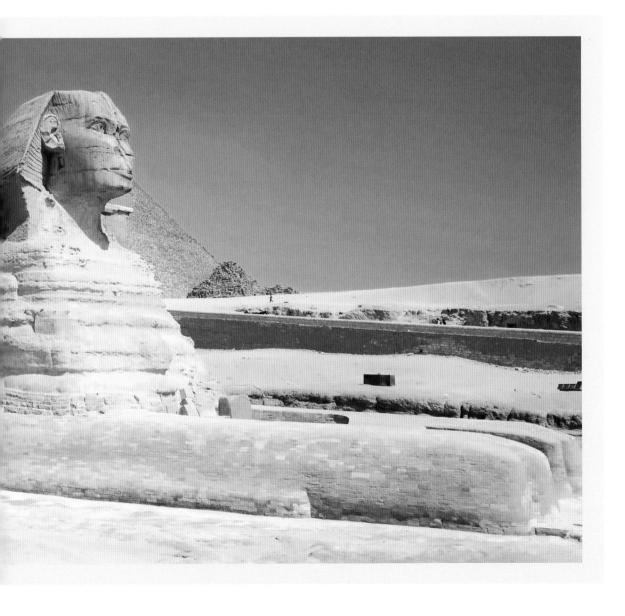

ABOVE: **Anat is often
depicted with a shuttle,
associating her with
Neith, Egyptian goddess
of weaving and war.**

an inevitable and common consequence of one mythological character being absorbed into another culture and belief system across expanses of land and sea, and centuries of time. A sphinx myth from Egypt, probably from the New Kingdom, shows this point, as it forms a stark contrast to that of Boeotian Thebes.

Yam, Canaan's god of chaos, meets Set of Egypt

A change in narrative through the influence of Ancient Egypt's mythology is shown in the epic tale of the Canaanite god, Yam. First, though, comes the original tale from the region.

Yam, whose name means 'sea', was the Canaanite god of chaos, of rivers and, of course, the seas, especially tempestuous ones. In one myth, the high god El grants Yam divine kingship and sovereignty over all other gods. Yam is pleased and all is well for a while. Soon, though, power goes to his head, his ruthless side surfaces, and he begins to oppress the other gods so much that the mother goddess, Ashehra, wife of El, pleads with him to stop. Then, knowing her mistake and fearful of a backlash against her children, she offers herself to Yam.

This is too much for Baal, god of death and disease, who conspires with the great Council of Gods to hatch a rebellion against Yam. But El gets wind of it and demands that the Council arrest Baal and hand him over for punishment, which would mean certain death. Bravely, the gods refuse, and Baal slips away to arm himself with the most lethal weapons made by Kothar wa-Khasis, the god of craftspeople.

In a mighty battle, Baal defeats Yam and rescues Ashehra, but is turned on by Mot, the god of death and infertility. Mot murders Baal after accusing him of collateral damage in slaying not only Yam but also Lotan, a mighty sea serpent associated with him. As he lies lifeless, it seems that all is lost for Baal. But his sister-lover Anat restores him, bringing him fully to life. In doing so, Anat ensures also that the drought at the wane of the dry season ends, the rains come and crops can be sown. The annual cycle is assured and there is hope for the future.

The similarities with the story of Osiris, Isis and Set are evident. Moreover, with the exchange of ideas and cultures across the region, Ancient Egyptians became acquainted with Yam through the Astarte Papers, which refer to the goddess Astarte brought to Egypt by Hyksos settlers.

Therefore, Ancient Egyptians constructed another version of the Canaan myth in which it is the goddess Astarte who tries to persuade Yam to mend his ways, while mighty Set, god of the desert storm, is the hero who defeats him, in a rare positive portrayal (although early aspects of Set do portray him as morally upright, and as a friend of the dead; someone who gave them a helping hand up the ladder to heaven). In tune with the theme of renewal in the myth of Yam, Set is also a protector of desert oases, bringing water to parched land, just as Anat brings rain to Canaan.

There are other versions of this story and other parallels with Ancient Egyptian myths, as there are across the Levant and into north-central modern-day Turkey. From the second millennium BCE, this was the land of the Hittites, who invaded Ancient Egypt in 1274 BCE. Incomers of all kinds gifted their myths.

Amun and the arrival of the Hyksos

Amun, a creator deity and cult god of the city of Thebes, stayed out of the limelight, outshone by Montu, the fierce warrior god. As with other creator gods, Amun was hidden, mysterious and with an undefined malleable nature, capable of shape-shifting into any aspect or scenario that a prevailing ruler thought fit.

When Memphis became the capital of Egypt and Thebes became a comparative backwater for a while, Amun led a quiet life with his wife, Amunet. His cult priests and local nomarchs, however, had other ideas and started to build up Amun's image. By the Middle Kingdom (2055–1650 BCE), Amun had sidelined Amunet in favour of Mut, and created a son, Khonsu, the moon god. They all thrived until a period of political disruption, known as the Second Intermediate Period (1650–1550 BCE).

This may have been kickstarted by the arrival of Hyksos settlers at the port city of Avaris in the Lower Nile, or possibly the incomers were just filling a political vacuum. Gradually, by about 1720 BCE, these migrants of unknown origin (perhaps the Levant), rose to power in Lower Egypt, established

ABOVE: Astarte was the Canaanite Queen of Heavens who was honoured with libations and burnt offerings.

themselves in Avaris and Memphis, and turned the Upper Egypt city of Thebes into a backwater once more.

The rise of Set and the arrival of new gods

Set, the malicious deity of chaos and violence, became the cult god of choice for the Hyksos. This was despite the fact that there is little evidence that the Hyksos conquered Lower Egypt by force, or that they controlled the region entirely. Their reputation as bringers of the horse-drawn chariot, which might indicate the strength and intent of their military capability, is unproven. But the adoption of Set was a good move in subduing the local population with his wrath on the one hand and, on the other, demonstrating the Hyksos's intent to blend in and observe Ancient Egypt's belief system.

The Hyksos did not forget their own gods, and brought new members into the pantheon. It is easy to understand how Set was picked out by the Hyksos when we look at one of their own most favoured gods: Reshef. Like Set, he was fearsome; unlike Set, he was a soldier rather than a malicious schemer. Among other aspects, Reshef was a proper god of war and thunder. Unlike Set, too, he had a loyal family. One of his wives was Itum; the other was Kadesh: between them, they produced the god of fertility, Min, who had an epic career spanning the whole of Ancient Egypt's mythological history.

Reshef did not catch on immediately with all the locals: it was mainly the incomers who attended his cult temple in the city of Memphis, which, in a seemingly uncharacteristic act of aggression, the Hyksos had pummelled. It is possible that the

AMUN-RE: GOD OF SEAFARERS

From a bas-relief inscription discovered at the temple of Deyr al-Medinah, Amun-Re, the great god of the sun and resurrection, shows his care for the many seafarers of Ancient Egypt, and his outward-looking character.

'Pay homage to Amun-Re…he who lifted up the sky, who made heaven and earth and the waters…. Come to me, Amun the valiant, he who saves the shipwrecked: let me reach dry land.'

Amun-Re shows his invisible air-like aspect with his ostrich feather crown.

OPPOSITE: The god Montu, who was associated with the Hyksos god, Reshef, faces Horus.

MIN AND PAN

Min (below) was a survivor – one of the gods who never really fell out of favour, despite all the regime changes, wars and invasions. He was a creator sky god, god of the Eastern Desert, of virility and of linen. His emblem consisted of two arrows and a hook, and his symbol was a lettuce. During the Ptolemaic period (332–30 BCE), his aspect as a fertility god fused well with that of Pan, whose name then carried the qualities of Min. His cult was centred around Coptos and Akhmim, on the eastern bank in Upper Egypt. The name Akhmim is said to derive from Khent-Min and Coptic Khmin. According to the Greek geographer Strabo (born 63 BCE), it became a great centre of linen, which enhanced the reputation of the god.

Hyksos formed a new class above their subjects in this highly stratified society; if so, their temple to Reshef may have been out of bounds to everyone but the wealthiest Ancient Egyptians.

This did not stop Reshef from growing in popularity among the locals. He formed a good example of the inculturation of gods from other lands: he became associated with Montu, the Theban war god, and rose to the position of 'Lord of Eternity' or 'Lord of the Sky'. At Giza, Amenhotep II (1426–1400 BCE) erected a stele of Reshef and Astarte to protect him as he prepared for war.

Reshef's physical image became a fusion of religious cultures. He is seen sporting a Syrian-style beard of the times, holding a spear, a battle-axe and a shield, with a Hittite gazelle head adorning the crown of Upper Egypt, his adopted homeland.

Reshef, god of plague

Reshef's Hebrew name, 'god of the plague' or 'flame god', might give us clues to his arrival in Avaris. It is not known exactly, but it is suggested that the Hyksos might have been driven from their homelands by plague. On the other hand, it is thought that Ancient Egypt's Middle Kingdom collapse around 1560 BCE might have been caused by plague and that the Hyksos merely took advantage of the calamity. Either way, Ancient Egyptians came to rely on Reshef to protect them from deadly epidemics, and from 'akha', a wicked spirit that caused stomach cramps.

One deity who was taken to the hearts of the locals was Astarte, a highly rated deity in the Middle East and the islands of the Mediterranean. Goddess of fertility, beauty and love, she bore that classic ambiguity of Ancient Egyptian gods in her other aspect as a goddess of war. She became identified with Hathor and Isis, both great mother goddesses, full of power and resolution. Astarte never became one of the greatest deities, but she was certainly international, and her cult following endured away from Ancient Egypt. In Cyprus, Phoenicians built many temples in her honour. Many other gods spread their wings.

Set, the god who slew his own brother Osiris and then chopped him into 13 pieces when his attempt to drown him failed, was responded to by Ancient Egyptians with both fear and fascination – their fear being expressed in the way they cut the ears off his statues, replacing them with Amun's ram horns (possibly in an attempt to reform him), or castrated him. That there were glimpses of a more protective side to Set made him slightly ambiguous and unnerving. Despite his sadistic violence, he stood the test of time and lasted all the way to the end of the kingdom.

The cult of Set spread beyond national boundaries. In Ancient Greece, he was identified with the monstrous god Typhon, who was inescapable, as his arms could stretch from the furthest point east to the furthest point west. The supreme god Zeus could only try to destroy Typhon by picking up fiery Mount Etna and hurling it at him.

ABOVE: A statue of Reshef (c. 1184-664 BCE) shows him in warfare mode, with a gazelle on his white crown.

Amun, the unlikely hero

In spite of the Hyksos and the threat of new gods, Amun would not lie down. When Ahmose I (c. 1570–1544 BCE) rose to subdue the Hyksos, the new pharaoh accredited the Theban cult god with his success, which ushered in the New Kingdom (1550–1069 BCE). Amun was a colourless cult god no longer, but was syncretized with the dazzling sun god Re to become Amun-Re. At last Amun had a visible presence: the simple, radiant shape of a sun disc.

Amun, together with the stalwarts Set, Osiris, Isis and Horus, were the main gods who stood the test of time throughout Ancient Egypt's history. In one form or another, they were taken across Europe by the Romans as they expanded their empire. Amun-Re, when exhibiting his aspect as a man wearing a loincloth and a two-feathered headdress, did not get much attention beyond Ancient Egypt. But as a ram-headed god, his cult spread along trade routes southward to Meroe in Sudan, and across the Mediterranean to Greece, where he became known as Ammon. Alexander the Great from Macedonia (ruled Egypt 332–323 BCE) consulted an oracle at Siwa oasis, who closely resembled Amun-Re's oracle at his cult centre at Thebes.

So what of incomers such as Reshef? Their stars could easily have waned. However,

OPPOSITE: The myth of Osiris and Set shows Osiris (left) lured into a beautiful coffin.

BELOW: The oracle at Siwa is said to have declared Alexander, 'son of Ammon'.

ALEXANDER A SACERD·APPELLAT·FIL·IOV·HAMM·

THE REPORT OF WENAMUN

The Report of Wenamun, a literary text in hieratic script, is a good example of how gods, myths, travel and politics were interconnected. Amun-Re, as a supreme god, is the reason why the tale emerged in the first place. The story was written between about 1090 and 1075 BCE, as Egypt's power in the eyes of its neighbours was waning and as Herihor took power.

The tale is a first-person narrative of a voyage from Egypt to the Levant to source wood for the ceremonial barque of Amun-Re at Thebes. The narrator describes his fantastical journey to the king on his return, and unfolds increasing obstacles to his mission as a result of Egypt's loss of power and status. The narrative includes invocations to gods, and their miraculous works, but also the trials of being robbed by pirates, and the cut and thrust of life on the high seas, as Wenamun in turn becomes the robber.

RIGHT: Wenamun faces the gods Horus, Anubis and Thoth as he narrates his tale on this Theban stele (c. 1075–925 BCE).

gods such as these already had an age-old mythological base in
the Middle East and the Mediterranean that never went away.
Their rise in Ancient Egypt, with its extensive trading networks
and imperial designs on its neighbours, could not have done
Reshef and others any harm. He became associated with the
great Greek god Apollo, and occasionally with the warring god
Mars, and even Rudra, the Rigvedic god of storms from the
Indian subcontinent, and Nergal, the Babylonian god of death
and disease.

LEFT: **A granite Ram
of Amun-Re statue
shields and endorses
King Taharqa
(690–664 BCE),
a Kushite ruler
from Nubia.**

Amun falls to Aten

The Great Hymn to Aten, the sun god, is rather like a biblical psalm. Some historians say that the sudden attempt at monotheism in Ancient Egypt is mirrored in biblical texts, to the extent that the Hebrew Shema prayer from the Torah can be found in the hymn. Time will tell whether or not this is true, but when Amenhotep IV decided to become Akhenaten, and to ditch all but the smallest gods in favour of Aten, a new concept of a single creator god emerged, even if it lasted for only 17 years.

As Akhenaten, 'One Who is Beneficial to Aten', this king was an iconoclast, smashing temples and statues of all other great gods. In their place, he built grand open-air temples, at first in Karnak. These sandstone block temples with covered walkways were lined with decorated pillars supporting massive statues of Akhenaten. Wall reliefs and paintings depicted this god king and his family bathed in the rays of Aten's blistering sunlight. Tiny hands at the tips of the rays reached out to Queen Nefertiti and her children, fusing them all with the bounty and blessings of Aten and the sun itself, which touched them with light and life.

No one knows why Akhenaten lurched so far from polytheism, except that maybe he was a desperate man, having no appetite for war or diplomacy and ambivalent to his neighbours, even his vassal states. Perhaps his lack of attention to matters of state was due to his myopic focus on Aten, which did not allow for anything else.

In the end, monotheism was a short trip. After Akhenaten's death, the deities and their myths re-emerged very quickly. Even Aten survived, none the

OPPOSITE: Queen Tey, behind King Ay (1323–1319 BCE), pays homage near the Hymn to Aten carved in Ay's Tomb, Amarna.

BELOW: King Akhenaten and Queen Nefertiti, on painted stone, bear their rearing cobra crowns of power.

worse for wear. Gods of old, those who had slid seamlessly into the system, and the myths and values attached to them, were only temporarily usurped. The old order, as mandated by Ma'at, was restored.

Shu and Tefnut: the lions that travelled

Aten, as represented by the sun disc, was also the solar aspect of Shu, the eldest son of the sun god. This association prevented Shu from being sidelined along with Amun during Akhenaten's reign. Palaces but not temples were honoured with Shu's name, and he owned a cultural centre at Nay-ta-hut where he and his wife, Tefnut, were worshipped as lion and lioness gods.

The Greeks renamed the city Leontopolis because of the gods' great following there, and fostered a myth in which Shu and Tefnut played together as lion cubs. As they grew into mature lions, Shu and Tefnut prowled the eastern and western borders of their territory to protect it. As fearsome defenders of the realm,

BELOW: Shu (left), not as a lion, wears a feather crown as his air aspect, while Tefnut wears a solar disc crown with uraei.

they were favoured as icons on either side of headrests, protecting
a person as they slept.

Melded with the god Akeru, meaning 'he who bends', or as
Ruti, 'the two lions', Shu was favoured by both Romans and
Greeks. These fierce icons protected the east and the west of
the underworld, especially Re as he embarked on his night-
time journey. Throughout, the lions carried Re on their backs,
defending him against the snake god, Apep, and against any foes
in the east at the point of sunrise. Greeks and Romans were keen
to have the two lions carved on either side of doorways. On their
hieroglyph, the two great cats were depicted at the extremities of
the horizon, often with spotted skin, like the extinct Barbary lion.

ABOVE: Depicted as
a lion pair on this
ivory neck stool from
Tutankhamun's tomb,
they are known as Ruti,
or 'Two Lions'.

Isis, a goddess who travels well

By the end of the Roman period in 395 CE, when the province
of Egypt became part of the Byzantine Empire, the pantheon
had dwindled to a number of high-profile gods, one of whom
was Isis, and her husband, Osiris. It is hard to know exactly what

characteristics helped a particular deity to survive among those of other cultures. One would be a strong myth that involved struggle, death and rebirth. Another would be an association with highly visible natural phenomena, such as the River Nile and the sun.

Legends and fairy stories: the growth of fiction

The myths of gods and goddesses are the most enduring literary heritage that we have of Ancient Egypt, associated as they are with the tangible and the visible: mystical hieroglyphs, stele, statues, temples, pyramids, and all manner of artefacts that reinforce the power of the stories with their heroes, heroines and foes. Yet there are other tales, written mostly from the New Kingdom (1550–1069 BCE) onwards, that resemble more, in their construction and cast, a prototype of the fairy-tale novel, rather like Arabia's *Tales from the Thousand and One Nights*.

Gods and goddesses still feature in these, but their lives are entwined with those of people rather than just each other, or divine kings. Cosmic tales come down to earth, and the gods become part of a cast that still involves kings and queens but as paupers, demons and more fairylike princesses. In their day, they might have been part of popular culture, and might have travelled well, influencing the form of legends and epics in other parts of the world. One such story involves Isis, a brave goddess of power, passion and clemency, whose attributes are shown in the tale below.

BELOW: Isis adopted Hathor's symbols and traits, like the colour turquoise, here on Isis's hair.

Isis and the seven scorpions

Isis and her husband Horus were hiding in a thick papyrus plantation by the Nile, safe from the sharp eyes of their persecutor, Set. Every evening, Isis took an evening stroll, accompanied by seven scorpion sentries. Three scorpions went ahead to check that all was clear; two watched her back, and two more walked by her side. Isis reminded her guards to walk quietly in case Set was nearby, and not to talk to strangers, lest they accidentally reveal Isis's name.

One night, they strolled towards Two Sisters Town, with the still waters of the Nile Delta shimmering around them. Needing a rest, they stopped on the outskirts of the town at the smart home of a noblewoman. But on seeing the scorpions and a woman whose rank and reputation she did not know, she slammed the door in their faces, leaving the scorpions writhing with rage, their vicious stinging tails curled upwards. Moving past the grand house, the tired party came upon the simple sunbaked-brick and reed-roofed home of a young peasant girl, who came out and offered them shelter for a while. Isis entered gladly but her loyal guards could not let their anger go.

One of the rearguard scorpions, Tefen, silently syphoned the venom from his comrades and filled his stinger. Quietly, he tiptoed away and made for the noblewoman's home, crawling through a gap under the front door. There, he found her son, fast asleep, and

BELOW: Isis is depicted with a serpent eating its own tail (uroborus), symbolizing eternity.

with no mercy, stung him with the powerful poison of seven scorpions. The little boy screamed, his mother rushed in, scooped him up and ran through the streets of the town, shouting for help for her child, who was on the point of death.

Isis, from inside the peasant girl's home, with the ears and senses of a goddess, heard the mother's cry, and forgetting the insult that Isis had received at the noblewoman's hands, ran out and took the boy, cradling him in her arms. Isis looked sternly at her scorpion sentries and named them out loud, one by one: Tjetet, Matet, Petet, Mesetet, Mesetetef, Befen, and finally, the main culprit, Tefen. As she named each of them, their poison became powerless and by the time Tefen's name was uttered, the boy was cured and free of pain (for scorpion stings are very painful). The noblewoman was so grateful for her son's life that she offered the hospitable peasant girl and Isis all her wealth, though Isis was above these things.

For many hundreds of years after the fall of Ancient Egypt first to the Greeks, and then the Romans, its gods and goddesses syncretized with those of the new rulers and imparted the spirit of their many aspects, which travelled far into the Middle East and Western Europe. But nothing could have prepared Ancient Egyptian deities for the cultural impact that revived in the nineteenth century and that continues to this day.

Myths in time

Ancient Egypt's myths have changed over time, and gods and goddesses have risen and fallen in favour with individual rulers or entire dynasties. Without a historical timeline to pin dates to known periods and rulers, scholars would have found it hard to assess their relevance or to establish pivotal points of change.

When Alexander the Great was invited to the Kingdom of Egypt to relieve it of its Persian oppressors, he heralded in the Ptolemaic period, which lasted from 332 to 30 BCE. The powerful influence of Greece was evident. Even Cleopatra VII (51–30 BCE) was not a native Egyptian but a Macedonian. Luckily, though, Greek philosophers, historians and writers, including Manetho, Plutarch and Herodotus, turned their attention to Ancient Egypt's belief system and mythology.

In the Ptolemaic period, Egyptian gods and goddesses became absorbed into the Greek pantheon. In the Roman era, these beliefs spread throughout the Roman Empire, often through the medium of mystery plays, such as that of Osiris. Some ancient ideas are still echoed in Coptic Christian Egypt, but the spread of Ancient Egypt's cosmology further afield can probably be best exemplified by the cult of Isis, which fanned out eastward to the Middle East, and westward to the shores of the Rhine, to Rome and, at its greatest extremity, to England.

RIGHT: A late statue (117–138 CE) of Isis appears as a Roman goddess, but shakes an Egyptian sistrum.

7

GOD AND MYTH AFTER THE FALL OF ANCIENT EGYPT

When Greeks took control of Ancient Egypt in 332 BCE, the old order in its pantheon was shaken. Under Greece, and then Rome, the deities of Ancient Egypt were melded and reshaped. But because these great empires were so far-reaching, Egypt's gods and goddesses enjoyed extraordinary longevity.

Sunk in the silt of the Nile Delta

Set, the god of chaos and destruction, must have been delighted. Seismic movements in the southern Mediterranean had undermined the great city port of Thonis-Heracleion, home to a great temple to Amun. Once the only port entry to Egypt from the Greek world, this was a pivotal trading station from about the eighth century BCE. But following the tremors and other

OPPOSITE: **The second mummiform coffin from Tutankhamun's tomb shows the king as Osiris, with vulture and cobra patterned arms.**

natural disasters, the silt mound of creation that lay beneath the city churned over time, then dissolved through a process of liquefaction and subsidence.

Great granite statues of the gods, like Hapi, god of the Nile, who guarded the entry to the port, slid slowly into the muddy waters, where rising seas covered them until they were discovered only in 2000 lying 45m (150ft) beneath the surface of Egypt's Bay of Aboukir. The symbolic slide of this great port mirrored that of Ancient Egypt as it ceded power and began to crumble. Yet all was not lost where the seas rose.

Gods, goddesses, their myths and symbols spread beyond Egypt through trade, which expanded rapidly after the transformational opening of the Silk Road around 130 BCE. Alexandria became a pivotal port, linking East and West, from where Egyptian culture could spread beyond the bounds of the Mediterranean and Middle East. Deities such as the goddess Isis became known as far as Afghanistan to the east.

Many Ancient Egyptian structures and monuments collapsed – not as a result of natural disaster, but more out of neglect, plunder and the sands of the desert, which reclaimed their realm. In the early days of the Roman Empire, obelisks, steles, sphinxes and statues to the gods were transported to the Italian heartland, where they were erected by the powerful, from popes to generals, only to fall out of favour once more. The gods and goddesses of Ancient Egypt had been forgotten, subsumed by the great monotheisms of the Middle East.

Resurrecting gods and myths

During the Renaissance period in Europe, the worlds of the ancient Mediterranean civilizations opened up to scholars through newly discovered writings. Excavations began in Italy that unearthed not only great artefacts and monuments from the Classical world but a surprising number of Ancient Egyptian finds as well. This revelation kickstarted an obsession with Ancient Egypt's material culture, mysticism and pantheon.

By the late eighteenth century, Ancient Egypt's tombs and temples became regular destinations for wealthy tourists and budding artists and architects, who spent their money on Grand Tours of Europe, which now included the eastern Mediterranean. In 1798, Napoleon tasked historians, scientists and other scholars to study the sites of Ancient Egypt while he went about his military campaign to secure the region for France. The campaign notoriously failed, but crucial finds, such as the Rosetta Stone, were unearthed. When in 1822 this stone became the key to unlocking the meaning of hieroglyphs, the mysteries of all other writings were revealed, and a swell of enthusiasm arose for Ancient Egyptian culture and beliefs.

Interest exploded in a new area of study: archaeology. By the beginning of the nineteenth century, the first Egyptologists dug up the possessions of kings and gods, first in a random way and then as a systematic discipline. A mania for all things Ancient Egyptian influenced Victorian design, from jewellery to architecture. During the Victorian era, everything from cotton mills to pumping stations and mausoleums to theatres bore forms and details that paid homage to the temples, shrines, obelisks

BASTET, THE CAT WHO TRAVELLED TO ROME

Bastet was one of Ancient Egypt's best-loved goddesses, and as such survived the fall of Ancient Egypt. Originally a ferocious goddess whose cult was centred on the Nile Delta at Bubastis, she also had a strong following in Memphis. During the New Kingdom (1550–1069 BCE), she softened, and was much loved as a protector of family and home. Many cats were ritually slaughtered in her name, and mass-produced bronze figurines attest to her popularity.

The Romans were so fond of Bastet, and respectful of her protective aspect, that they carried her to Italy, where her image has been found in Rome, Pompeii, Ostia and Nemi. Bastet is represented in many forms and was a popular subject for amulets. She can be shown as a woman with the head of a cat, wearing an expensive dress and carrying a bag on her arm. In her hand she carries a sistrum (an ancient percussive instrument), while her breastplate sports the head of a lioness.

RIGHT: A bronze figure of Bastet, cast from the sixth–fourth centuries BCE, shows her carrying a lion-headed shield.

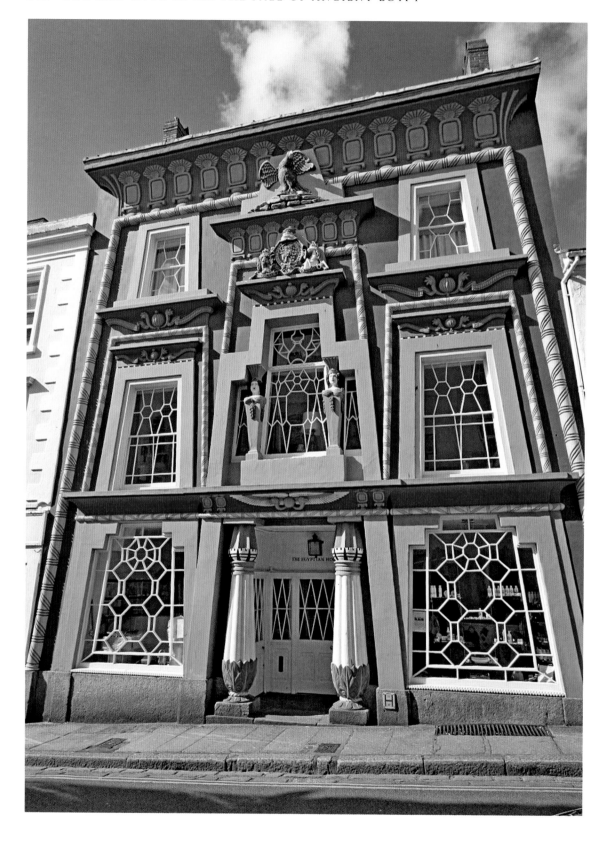

OPPOSITE: On the 1835 Egyptian House in England's Penzance port, lotus-bud capitals top door columns.

LEFT: Victorian 'Ancient Egyptian' jewellery includes a gold and turquoise scarab beetle bar brooch.

and steles dedicated to the gods and goddesses of Ancient Egypt. In France, the lotus flower, divine symbol of Ancient Egypt, became *the fleur de lis*.

The momentous discovery of Tutankhamun

In November 1922, when a young Egyptian boy led the British Egyptologist Howard Carter (1874–1939) to steps that went down into the tomb of Tutankhamun, a new frenzy of interest started. Carter could never have imagined the treasures and knowledge that he would uncover. Bound in with the bandages of Tutankhamun's mummified body were 143 small artefacts alone; amulets, glistening with gold and precious jewels.

Shaped with the symbols of gods and goddesses and imbued with the

BELOW: Tutankhamun's treasure included this gold winged-cobra collar amulet.

powers in myth that they represented, they included a winged headed collar for Nekhebet; a bracelet in the shape of an eye for Horus; a human-headed winged cobra as the goddess Meretseger, and boat-shaped pieces to represent Tutankhamun's journey into the underworld. To crown them all, under his helmet was found a golden diadem with the falcon and the serpent, the two symbols representing his godly right to rule both Upper and Lower Egypt.

Yet although interest in the discovery of Tutankhamun's tomb was acute, and Howard Carter's fame spread far and wide, there were surprising and intriguing finds relating to gods and goddesses closer to Carter's home, whose images, statues and inscriptions he could have studied. One of these was the goddesses, Isis.

LEFT: In 1926, Howard Carter and a colleague sit beside King Tutankhamun's coffin, carefully removing consecration oils that cover the third, innermost coffin.

Isis, international goddess

Under the Greeks, Isis, mother goddess, loyal wife and protector of all, became no less than a queen, with a new name, Eset, the Greek form of an early Egyptian word meaning 'throne'. Her reputation grew so great that she became a most potent goddess of magic, whose powers were stronger than those of her husband, Osiris, and even the sun god Re.

Temples dedicated to Isis, now also honoured as the goddess of seafarers, were scattered across the port city of Alexandria, where sailors, merchants, emissaries and officials spread her cult to Greece, then to Rome, where she became Isis-Aphrodite, the great mother goddess of fertility. Throughout Rome's extensive empire, Isis lived on, blending in wherever she touched down. Her influence did not die even when Greece and Rome turned to monotheistic Christianity: some art historians see a likeness between images of Isis cradling the baby Horus and early depictions of the Madonna and child. In spite of this pinnacle of legacies, Isis did not survive in literature as did her son, Horus.

BELOW: **Isis was worshipped at Isis Philae temple until 550 CE. It was the last temple built in classical Egyptian style.**

ISIS REACHES LONDON

'*Londini ad Fanum Isidis*' ('To London at the Temple of Isis').
This roughly inscribed direction to Isis's temple in London on a
first-century CE Roman flagon was unearthed under Tooley Street in
the borough of Southwark. Small bronze figurines, lead weights and
a hairpin all with Isis's name or in her likeness gave further proof
that Isis reigned in London. Finally, set in a Roman wall built along
the River Thames was found a temple altar from the third century
CE, with the inscription, 'The temple had fallen down through old
age, but had been restored'. Unfortunately, the temple had not been
restored well enough to survive.

Horus in Victorian English literature

Horus, falcon god of creation and unifier of Upper and Lower
Egypt, did not endlessly circle a broken empire. His diverse
aspects and ambiguous roles as both father and son of Osiris
made him a flexible god whose mythological status was ripe for
turning into a great literary character. This was not lost on the
Victorian novelist H. Rider Haggard (1856–1925), who opted
for Harmachis, or 'Horus in the Horizon', an aspect of Horus
not often mined.

The cult of Harmachis centred around the Great Sphinx
on the Giza Plateau. Although his aspect was generally positive,
it is said that builders from the Levant who were working
near the Sphinx mistook the name of his temple, 'Harmachis
Hauron' for Hauron, their god of terror. This is perhaps why
his fictional character is less than the exemplary Horus of
traditional myth.

Horus, as well as being a god, was also manifested bodily
in Egyptian kings through the ages; it is this concept that
Haggard ran with in his 1889 novel, *Cleopatra: Being An
Account Of The Fall And Vengeance Of Harmachis,
The Royal Egyptian, As Set Forth By His Own Hand.*

The novel is set in Ptolemaic times. Harmachis is urged
by high priests of the cult of Isis, mother of Horus, and the
citizens of Egypt, to assassinate Queen Cleopatra VII
(51–30 BCE) and seize the throne. It is only Harmachis who,

BELOW: **A bronze
statuette shows Isis
nursing her son Horus,
with a powerful solar
disc crown.**

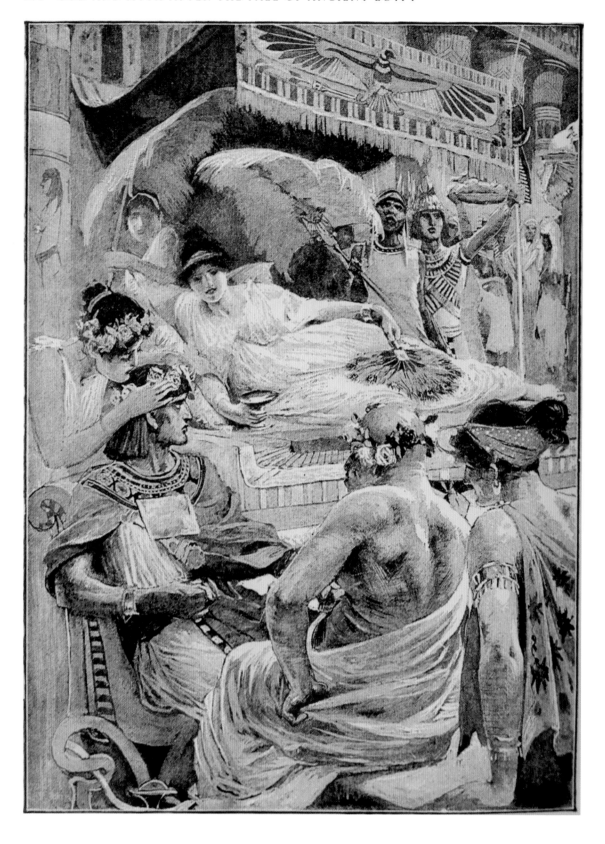

as the direct descendant of the first king of Egypt, shares the royal blood and link with the gods, and it is only in this way that the Greeks and Romans will be expelled. The proud empire of Ancient Egypt would be restored under its rightful king. Cleopatra, who was descended from Macedonian kings, was considered an upstart incomer with no biological or godly right to the throne.

However, Harmachis's mission collapses as he falls in love with this beguiling and astute queen, leaving the high priests, the people, and Isis, mother and queen of all goddesses, feeling betrayed, and Ancient Egypt on the slide. The novel, in several volumes, had mixed reviews at the time, but was one of countless books, plays and eventually films about the ultimate femme fatale, Cleopatra, and the belief system that upheld her position.

The fascination with Cleopatra has extended into modern times to other aspects of Ancient Egypt's rich cultural past. From the 2018 film *Scorpion King: Book of Souls* to computer games such as *Assassin's Creed Origins* and *Egyptian Senet*, a mystical journey into the afterlife based on senet, the Ancient Egyptian board game, gods, goddesses and their myths can be seen as constantly evolving in popular culture. The process of reinvention does not look likely to stop.

New tools to uncover more myths

Wepwawet, the jackal-headed 'opener of the ways', who allowed the deceased to breathe, eat, speak and smile in the afterlife and their complex souls to circulate, must have been delighted at the invention of a new investigative gadget. Named after him, Upuaut is a tiny robot used to investigate airshafts in the Great Pyramid.

This is just one of a number of modern techniques used to discover more about Ancient Egypt's history and belief system. At the University of Zurich, Roger Seiler and Frank Ruhli have advanced the craniological study of mummies, using a radiological procedure, computed tomography, which allows the skull to be scanned without disturbing the mummy's wrappings.

Meanwhile, from space, like the eyes of a cosmic god, infrared technology is being used to map pyramids and settlements covered by desert sands.

Kemetic Orthodoxy, a faith with Ancient Egyptian roots

A new faith with Ancient Egypt's gods, goddesses and narratives at its heart emerged in the 1980s, led by Reverend Tamara L. Siuda. Known as Kemetic Orthodoxy, it is a faith, community and culture based on traditional African beliefs featuring more than one deity and synchronized pairs of gods and goddesses. Reverend Siuda is known as Her Holiness but also as Nisut-bityt:

OPPOSITE: Cleopatra manipulates her enemy, Harmachis, on this plate taken from H. Rider Haggard's 1894 novel.

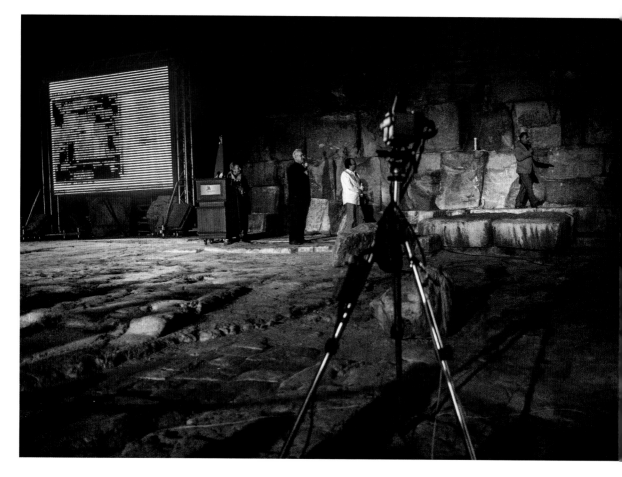

ABOVE: **An infrared thermography experiment maps out wall temperatures at Giza's Pyramid of Khufu in 2015.**

OPPOSITE: (Top) Sumerian tablet of accounts (2350 BCE). (Bottom) List of Kings from 'before the flood' to 1817 BCE.

She of the Sedge and the Bee – in other words, from both Upper and Lower Egypt. She is seen by her followers not as a goddess but as a human intermediary between people and deities, although she is invested with the royal *ka*, or spirit, of Heru, a form of the sky god Horus. Daily rituals begin with the Rite of the House of the Morning, honouring the rising sun. Followers are also obliged to honour Akhu, the spirits of the ancestors, who must be respected.

Ancient Egypt's mythology compared

We have seen how Ancient Egypt's myths at times synchronized with those of the Levant and Mesopotamia. Comparisons have been made with the mythology of the Mesopotamian kingdom of Sumer, which, since 4000 BCE, had been home to deities such as Enhil, god of wind and storm; Utu, god of justice and the sun; and his father Nanna, god of the moon, and where pyramid-like ziggurats became temples. Like the great myth of Osiris and Set, the Sumerian *Epic of Gilgamesh* wrestles with murder and immortality, although their narratives diverge. Like Ancient Egypt too, many of Sumer's mysteries lie unfathomed, with most of its 50,000 inscribed clay tablets still untranslated.

Harmony and balance in Ancient China

Ancient China's two great predynastic creation myths, The Three Sovereigns and The Five Emperors, predate real emperors, who ruled from around 2000 BCE, and who adopted godly status. As with Ancient Egypt, there were creation myths around the cosmic egg, in which the sky and earth were not separated until a human form, P'an Ku, grew as Earth separated from Sky, filling the void between them until, after 18,000 years, Earth and Sky reached their proper distance. P'an Ku died, and his scattered body parts formed the celestial bodies and the natural elements of the world: mountains and valleys, rivers and seas, clouds and wind, minerals, and humankind. As with Ma'at, the role of P'an Ku was one of harmony and balance.

In a Yangtze Delta tradition, P'an Ku and his wife, Nu Kua, are like the two parts of an egg, representing balance as two opposite forces: yin and yang, working together, like water and fire, the moon and the sun. Some believe that the heavens are yang, an upturned bowl revolving on a pivotal axis with stars attached to it, while Earth, the yin, lies below as a one-dimensional square or a truncated four-sided pyramid.

China's ancient belief system boasted its own rich pantheon of deities for the cosmos, such as the Moon Goddess, Heng-o; or of earthly places, such as Hsi Wang Mu, Royal Mother

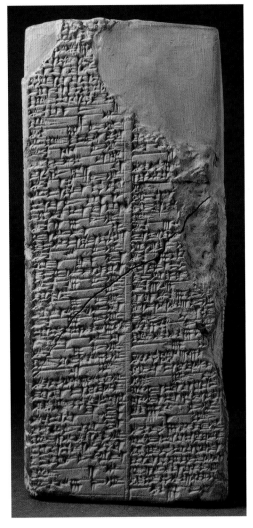

RIGHT: **P'an Ku holds**
the cosmic egg with
its yin and yang
symbol of harmony
on an eighteenth
century lithograph.

of the Western Paradise; and of farming, science and skill,
such as Shen-nung, the creator of agriculture and medicine.
China's mythological past, though, is also incomplete due to
an overzealous government minister, Li Szu, who persuaded the
first emperor of a united China, Qin Shi Huang (259–210 BCE),
to destroy original tellings of the myths and reinterpret them
through later religions, Confucianism and Taoism, which
blended better with the politics of the time.

Nature, faith and humankind

As an African mythology, Ancient Egypt's sits well with others
on the continent, where, among many other deities, water
goddesses of West African kingdoms and the belief by some of
southern Africa's hunter-gatherer groups that the dead become
stars make the link between nature, belief and humankind.

Upepo, the Swahili word for wind, also means the spirit, and
in Maasai, Orpeko is the ethereal, invisible force that disrupts
bodies, minds and lives. Ancient belief systems and myths across
much of the continent hold to the complex and grand idea that
nature and the heavens work together with earthlings and the
ancestors, interrupted at times by spirits both benign and malign.
This belief system might chime with the indigenous people
of Australia.

For at least 30,000 years, Indigenous Australians have
mapped the spiritual and physical landscape of what is the largest
island in the world. Using the word 'mapped' is not figurative,
but an accurate description of the way in which individual totems
and their myths link with each other in chains that criss-cross
deserts and mountains; rivers and creeks. Each person carries
with them their own clan totem, with its unique story revealed

BELOW: Indigenous
Australian rock art
at Ubirr, Kakadu,
Northern Territory,
shows animal and
plant totems.

in song, drama and millions of artworks that adorn and identify the rock outcrops and other landscape features of this country. Together, the narratives of the totems link the heavens of creation with the earth, and all nature within it. Yet, when sung, they offer a practical route that will enable a traveller to survive a journey across Australia's challenging landscapes. The gods, goddesses, kings, queens and peoples of Ancient Egypt would surely have understood this, not least the god Osiris.

The legacy of the risen Osiris in Christianity

The last word goes to Osiris, whose likeness was symbolically buried and resurrected every year in a ceremony to ensure the renewal of nature, a good harvest, and the perpetuation of the kingdom. By burying likenesses of the god fashioned from soil and seed, and by watering them for eight days until the wheat and barley sprouted, priests ensured that life would spring

BELOW: At the Temple of Seti I at Abydos, a relief depicts the resurrection of Osiris, with Isis and falcon god Sokar.

eternal in all ways and for all living beings. In the great temples, another seed statuette, and one fashioned from ground-up precious stones were paraded through the temple; one a symbol of the renewal of nature, the other, a symbol of Osiris's everlasting, sparkling stellar power.

E.A. Wallis Budge (1857–1934), whose translations of myths and legends have been adapted in this book, likened the life, death and meaning of Osiris with that of Jesus Christ in his 1911 work *Osiris and the Egyptian Resurrection*. He points out that the ideas of a spiritual being who suffered on earth, was resurrected from the dead, became judge of the words and deeds of humankind, and who ruled a heaven filled only with sinless beings, are as old as dynastic Egypt. In this extract, he looks at the Osiris cult from a believer's point of view:

'The central point of each Osirian's religion was his hope of resurrection in a transformed body and of immortality, which could only be realised by him through death and resurrection of Osiris.'

The depth and complexity of Ancient Egypt's belief system may never truly be understood, nor will we manage to unpick the woven tapestry of all the gods, goddesses, their aspects, and the messages in their myths. Yet we do not give up trying. Perpetual striving is the daily bread of Osiris, who, as with nature, keeps dying and reviving; nothing will keep him down.

From Spell 330, Coffin Texts

'Whether I live or die I am Osiris

I enter in and reappear through you,

I decay in you, I grow in you,

I fall down in you, I fall upon my side.

The gods are living in me for I live and grow in the corn

that sustains the honoured one.

I cover the earth,

whether I live or die I am Barley.

I am not destroyed....'

Ancient Egypt's King List (reigns)

Historians are unsure of exact dates of kings, so all are approximations, but a king list gives a reference point for rulers and dynasties. Upper and Lower Egypt and some regions were ruled by different kings at certain times. A wife, son or daughter might rule at the same time as a king. Alternative dates are given in some instances.

Early Dynastic Period

Dynasty 1 (circa 3150–2890 BCE)

Legendary king or kings, whose names included Narmer, Menes and Scorpion, began the unification of Ancient Egypt from around at least 3150 BCE. The following 'Horus' kings ascended in this order as so far known. Aha, Djer, Djet, Den, Anedjib, Semerkhet, Qa'a

Dynasty 2 (2890–2686/2649 BCE)

Hetepsekhemwy, Raneb, Nynetjer, Weng and Seneg, Peribsen, Khaasekhemwy

Old Kingdom

Dynasty 3 (2686/2649–2575/ 2160 BCE)

Sanakht (2686/2649–2630)
Djoser (2667–2648/2630–2611)
Sekhemkhet (2611–2605)
Khaba (2605–2599)
Huni (2599–2575)

Dynasty 4 (2613/2575–2465 BCE)

Snefru (2575–2551)
Khufu (2551–2528)
Djedefre (2528–2520)
Khafre (2520–2494)
Nebka II (2494–2490)
Menkaure (2490–2472)
Shepseskaf (2472–2467)
Thamphthis (2467–2465)

Dynasty 5 (2494/2465–2323 BCE)

Userkaf (2465–2458)
Sahure (2458–2446)
Neferirkare (2446–2438)
Shepseskare (2438–2431)
Neferefre (2431–2420)
Niuserre (2420–2389)
Menkauhor (2389–2381)
Isesi (2381–2353)
Unis (2353–2323)

Dynasty 6 2323–2181/2150 BCE

Teti (2323–2291)
Userkare (2291–2289)
Pepi I (2289–2255)
Merenre I (2255–2246)
Pepi II (2246–2152)
Merenre II (2152–2152)
Netjerkare Siptah (2152–2150)

First Intermediate Period (2181/2160–2055/ 2150–2030 BCE)

Dynasties 8–10 (2150–2030)

Little is known of rulers during this period.

Dynasty 11 (first half 2124– 2030 BCE)

Mentuhotep I (2124–2120)
Intef I (2120–2108)
Intef II (2108–2059)
Intef III (2059–2051)
Mentuhotep II (2051–2030)

Middle Kingdom (2055–1650/2030–1640 BCE)

Dynasty 11 (second half 2030– 1981 BCE)

Mentuhotep II (cont. 2030–2000)
Mentuhotep III (2000–1988)
Qakare Intef (1985–1985)
Sekhentibre (1985–1985)
Menekhkare (1985–1985)
Mentuhotep IV (1988–1981)

Dynasty 12 (1981–1802 BCE)

Amenemhat I (1981–1952)
Senusret I (1961–1917)
Amenemhat II (1919–1885)
Senusret II (1887–1878)
Senusret III (1875–1855/1878– 1840)
Amenemhat III (1859–1813)
Amenemhat IV (1814–1805)
Nefrusobek (1805–1802)

Dynasty 13 (1802–1640 BCE)

Second Intermediate Period (1650–1550/1640–1540 BCE)

Dynasties 14–16 1640–1635 BCE)

Dynasty 17 (1635–1550 BCE)

Tao I (1560–?)
Tao II (1560–?)
Kamose (1552–1550)

New Kingdom (1550–1070 BCE)

Dynasty 18 (1550–1295 BCE)

Ahmose (1550–1525)
Amenhotep I (1525–1504)
Thutmose I (1525–1504/1514–1493)
Thutmose II (1492–1479)
Thutmose III (1479–1425)
Hatshepsut (as regent 1479–1473)
Hatshepsut (reigned 1473–1458)
Amenhotep II (1427–1400)
Thutmose IV (1400–1390)
Amenhotep III (1386–1353/1390–1352)
Amenhotep IV (1352–1349)
Akhenaten (1353/1349–1336)
Neferneferuaton (1338–?)
Smenkhkare (1336–?)
Tutankhamun (1336–1327)
Aya (1327–1323)
Haremhab (1323–1295)

Dynasty 19 (1295–1186 BCE)

Rameses I (1295–1294)
Seti I (1294–1279)
Rameses II (1279–1213)
Merneptah (1213–1203)
Amenmose (1203–1200)
Seti II (1200–1194)
Siptah (1194–1188)
Tawosret (1188–1186)

Dynasty 20 (1186–1070 BCE)

Sethnakht (1186–1184)
Rameses III (1187–1156/1184–1153)
Rameses IV (1153–1147)
Rameses V (1147–1143)
Rameses VI (1143–1136)

Rameses VII (1136–1129)
Rameses VIII (1129–1126)
Rameses IX (1102–1073/1099–
1075/1070)
Rameses X (1108–1099)
Rameses XI (1099–1070)

**High Priest rulers of Amun
(1080–1070 BCE)**
Herihor (1080–1074)
Paiankh (1074–1070)

Third Intermediate Period
(1066–664/1070–713 BCE)

Dynasty 21 (1070–945 BCE)
Smendes (1070–1044)

**High Priest rulers of the south
(1070–992 BCE)**
Pinedjem I (1070–1032)
Masaharta (1054–1046)
Djedkhonsefankh (1046–1045)
Menkheperre (1045–992)
Amenemnisu (1044–1040)
Psusennes I (1040–992)
Amenemope (992–984)
High Priest Smendes (992–990)
High Priest Painedjem II (990–969)
Osochor (984–978)
Siamun (978–959)
High Priest Psusennes (969–959)
Psusennes II (959–945)

Dynasty 22 (Libyan 945–712)
Sheshonq I (945–924)
Osorkon I (924–889)
Sheshonq II (890–?)
Takelot I (889–874)
Osorkon II (874–850)
Harsiese (865–?)
Takelot II (850–825)
Sheshonq III (825–773)
Pami (773–767)
Sheshonq V (767–730)
Osorkon IV (730–712)

Dynasty 23 (818–713 BCE)
Pedubaste I (818–793)
Iuput I (800–?)

Sheshonq IV (793–787)
Osorkon III (787–759)
Takelot III (764–757)
Rudamun (757–754)
Iuput II (754–712)
Peftjaubast (740–725)
Namlot (740–?)
Thutemhat (720–?)

Dynasty 24 (724–712 BCE)
Tefnakht (724–717)
Bakenrenef (717–712)

Late Period
(664–332/712–332 BCE)

Dynasty 25 (Nubian 712–664 BCE)
Piye (743–712)
Shabaqo (712–698)
Shebitqo (698–690)
Taharqo (690–664 Loses Lower Egypt)
Tanutamani (664–653 Loses Upper
Egypt)

Dynasty 26 (Saite 688–252 BCE)
Nikauba (688–672)
Necho I (672–664)
Psamtik I (664–610)
Necho II (610–595)
Psamtik II (595–589)
Apries (589–570)
Amasis (570–526)
Psamtik III (526–525)

Dynasty 27 (Persian 525–404 BCE)
Cambyses (525–522)
Darius I (521–486)
Xerxes I (486–466)
Artaxerxes I (465–424)
Darius II (424–404)

Dynasty 28 (522–399 BCE)
Pedubaste III (522–520)
Psamtik IV (470 –?)
Inaros (460–?)
Amyrtaios I (460–?)
Thannyros (445–?)
Pausiris (445–?)
Psamtik V (445–?)
Psamtik VI (400–?)

Amyrtaios I (404–399)

Dynasty 29 (399–380 BCE)
Nepherites I (399–393)
Psammuthi (393–?)
Achoris (393–380)
Nepherites II (380–?)

Dynasty 30 (380–343 BCE)
Nectanebo I (380–362)
Teos (365–360)
Nectanebo II (360–343)

Persian Period (343–332 BCE)

Khabebesh (343–332)
Artaxerxes III Ochus (343–338)
Arses (338–336)
Darius III Codoman (335–332)

(Greek) Macedonian Period
(332–304 BCE)

Alexander the Great (332–332)
Philip Arrhidaeus (323–316)
Alexander IV (316–304)

(Greek) Ptolemaic Period
(330/304–30 BCE)

Ptolemy I Soter I (304–284)
Ptolemy II Philadelphos (285–246)
Arsinoe II (278–270)
Ptolemy III Euergetes I (246–221)
Berenike II (246–221)
Ptolemy IV Philopator (222–205)
Ptolemy V Epiphanes (205–180)
Harwennefer (205–199)
Ankhwennefer (199–186)
Cleopatra I (194–176)
Ptolemy VI Philometor (180–145)
Cleopatra II (175–115)
Ptolemy VIII Euergetes II (170–116)
Harsiese (130–?)
Ptolemy VII Neos Philopator (145–144)
Ptolemy IX Soter II (116–80)
Ptolemy XII (57–51)
Cleopatra VII (51–30)

Roman Period (30 BCE–395 CE)

Adapted from the King List from the Metropolitan Museum of Arts, Department of Egyptian Art, in the 'Heilbrunn Timeline of Art History'.

BIBLIOGRAPHY

Arnold, Dieter: *Temples of the Last Pharaohs* (Oxford University Press, 1999)

Brier, Dr Bob: *Ancient Egypt, Everyday Life in the Land of the Nile* (Sterling, 2013)

Budge, E.A.W.: *The Gods of the Egyptians, Two Volumes* (Dover, New York, 1969)

Budge, E.A.W.: *Legends of the Egyptian Gods* (Dover, New York, 1994)

Bunson, Margaret: *Encyclopedia of Ancient Egypt* (Gramercy Books, 1991)

Dunand, Francoise and Zivie-Coche, Christiane: *Gods and Men in Ancient Egypt* (Cornell University Press, 2004)

Dunand, Francoise and Lichtenberg, Roger: *Mummies and Death in Egypt* (Cornell University Press, 2005)

Frankfurter, David: Religion in Roman Egypt: *Assimilation and Resistance* (Princeton University Press, 1998)

Gibson, Clare: *The Hidden Life of Ancient Egypt* (Saraband, 2009)

Heller, Reinhold, Malek, Jaromir and Haddad, Nordine: *Egyptian Art (Art and Ideas)*, (Phaidon Press, 1999)

Meeks, David and Meeks, Christine Favard-Meeks: *Daily Life of the Egyptian Gods* (Pimlico, 1999)

Petrie, Sir William M. Flinders: *The Religion of Ancient Egypt* (Cosimo Classics, 2011)

Pinch, Geraldine: *Handbook of Egyptian Mythology* (Oxford University Press, 2004)

Sauneron, Serge, translated by Lorton, David: *The Priests of Ancient Egypt* (Cornell University Press, 2000)

Shaw, Ian: *The Oxford History of Ancient Egypt* (Oxford University Press USA, 2004)

Smith, William Stevenson and Simpson, William Kelly: *The Art and Architecture of Ancient Egypt* (Yale University Press, 1998)

Spence, Lewis: *Ancient Egyptian Myths and Legends* (Dover Publications, 1990)

Strudwick, Nigel, edited by Leprohon, Ronald J.: *Texts from the Pyramid Age (Writings from the Ancient World* (Society of the Biblical World, 2005)

Taylor, J.H.: Journey Through the Afterlife: *Ancient Egyptian Book of the Dead* (Tokyo, 2012)

Teeter, Emily: *Religion and Ritual in Ancient Egypt* (Cambridge Univeristy Press, 2011)

Tyldesley, Joyce: *The Penguin Book of Myths and Legends of Ancient Egypt* (Penguin UK, 2010)

Watterson, Barbara: *Gods of Ancient Egypt* (History Press, 2003)

Wilkinson, Richard: *The Complete Gods and goddesses of Ancient Egypt* (Thames and Hudson Ltd, 2017)

Wilkinson, Richard: *The Complete Temples of Ancient Egypt* (Thames and Hudson Ltd, 2017)

Wilkinson, Toby: *Writings from Ancient Egypt* (Penguin UK, 2016)

INDEX

PICTURE CREDITS

Alamy: 12 (BibleLandPictures.com), 18 (Alain Guilleux), 22 (Glasshouse Images), 25 (Prisma by Dukas Pressagentur), 30 (Interfoto), 32 (Magica), 36 (National Geographic Image Collection), 37 (Dinodia Photos), 38 (Panther Media), 42 (Interfoto), 43 (robertharding), 45 (Mike P Shepherd), 47 (National Geographic Image Collection), 48 (Interfoto), 49 (Lanmas), 54 (Classic Image), 64 (Kumar Sriskandan), 66 (The Picture Art Collection), 67 (Art Directors & Trip), 69 (Really Easy Star), 70 top (Christine Osborne Pictures), 71 (Peter Horree), 72 right (Dallet-Alba), 82 (EmmPi Stock Images), 84 (Art Directors & Trip), 87 (National Geographic Image Collection), 90 (Lanmas), 91 top (Magica), 91 bottom (BibleLandPictures.com), 94/95 (Graham Mulrooney), 96 top (MCLA Collection), 98 (Stefano Ravera), 100 (Peter Barritt), 102 (Artokoloro Quint Lox), 103 (Charles Walker Collection), 106 (Magica), 109 (BibleLandPictures.com), 111 (Hemis), 122 top (Cultural Archive), 123 (Alfredo Garcia Saz), 124 (age footstock), 126 (Azoor Photo Collection), 128 (Interfoto), 131 (Stefano Ravera), 136 (Mike P Shepherd), 141 (Peter Horree), 142 (Art Directors & Trip), 143 (Chronicle), 145 (Really Easy Star/Toni Spagone), 146 (Chris Deeney), 148/149 (Artmedia), 151 (Mike P Shepherd), 152 (Peter Horree), 154 (Peter Horree), 156 (Science History Images), 161 (Chronicle), 162 (Peter Horree), 164 (Classic Image), 166 left (PvE), 168 (funkyfood London-Paul Williams), 170 (Mick Sharp), 171 (BibleLandPictures.com), 172 (nik wheeler), 173 (Classic Image), 175 (BibleLandPictures.com), 176 (Peter Horree), 180 (Juan Aunion), 182 (Chris Deeney), 183 (Ivy Close Images), 185 (Artokoloro Quint Lox), 186 (Ivy Close Images), 187 (The Picture Art Collection), 188 (Peter Horree), 190 (Mike P Shepherd), 191 (Peter Horree), 192 left (Ivy Close Images), 192 right (Chronicle), 193 (Images of Africa Photobank), 195 (Science History Images), 197 (Peter Horree), 198 (robertharding), 200 (Newscom), 203 top left (Jeremy Pembrey), 203 bottom (Ancient Art & Architecture), 204/205 (Everett Collection Inc), 206 (robertharding), 208 (FLHC p1), 211 top (Granger Historical Picture Archive), 212 (John Astor), 213 (Sheralee Stoll)

Alamy/Heritage Image Partnership: 11, 16, 20, 24, 33, 39, 52, 59, 81, 93, 99, 122 bottom, 130, 181, 201, 211 bottom

Alamy/Prisma Archivo: 34, 44, 51 top, 73, 75, 112, 115, 121, 133, 166 right, 177, 214

Alamy/ World History Achive: 8, 23, 26, 51 middle, 56, 60/61, 68, 72 left, 114, 118/119, 134, 194

Bridgeman Images: 21 & 27 (DeAgostini Picture Library), 53 (Deir el-medina, Thebes, Egypt), 63 (DeAgostini Picture Library), 101 (DeAgostini Picture Library/S.Vannini), 108 (British Museum/ DeAgostini Picture Library), 144 (Louvre/G.Dagli Orti/DeAgostini Picture Library), 147 (G.Dagli Orti/ DeAgostini Picture Library), 150 (Museo Civico Archeologico/DeAgostini Picture Library/A.Dagli Orti), 153 (DeAgostini Picture Library/A.Gorozzo), 157 (Papyrus Museum, Cairo/DeAgostini Picture Library), 203 top right (Harry Stern Collection, bequest of Kurt Stern), 207 (Brooklyn Museum of Art/ Museum Collection Fund)

British Museum Images: 96 bottom

Dreamstime: 6 (Amanda Lewis), 10 (Lu Yang), 35 (marcin ciesielski), 50 (Wisconsinart), 74 (Dejan Gileski), 78 (Evgeniy Fesenko), 80 (Waupee), 174 (Evgeniy Fesenko), 178/179 (Claudio Caridi)

Getty Images: 9 (DeAgostini/G.Dagli Orti), 17 (DeAgostini/C.Sappa), 40 (Yann Arthus-Bertrand), 51 bottom (Universal History Archive/UIG Via Getty), 57 (Werner Forman), 70 bottom & 76 (DeAgostini/G.Dagli Orti), 86 (DeAgostini/A.Jemolo), 88 & 89 (DeAgostini/G.Dagli Orti), 105 (Corbis/ Leemage), 113 top (Khaled Desouki), 113 bottom (DeAgostini/W.Buss), 132 (DeAgostini Picture Library), 137-139 all (Werner Forman), 155 top & bottom (Werner Forman), 158 (Print Collector), 167 (DeAgostini/G.Dagli Orti), 169 top (DeAgostini/G. Sioen), 169 bottom (Patrick Landmann), 184 & 189 (Heritage Images), 210 (Khaled Desouki)

Shutterstock: 127 (Calin Stan), 202 (RogerMechan)